MEDICARE

101

FROM **YOUR INITIAL ENROLLMENT PERIOD** TO **PARTS A, B, C,** AND **D,** AN **ESSENTIAL PRIMER ON THE** GOVERNMENT HEALTHCARE PROGRAM

KIMBERLY LANKFORD

Adams Media

New York Amsterdam/Antwerp London Toronto
Sydney/Melbourne New Delhi

To Houman and Will

Aadamsmedia

Adams Media
An Imprint of Simon & Schuster, LLC
100 Technology Center Drive
Stoughton, MA 02072

First Adams Media hardcover edition February 2026

ADAMS MEDIA and colophon are registered trademarks of Simon & Schuster, LLC.

For information about special discounts for bulk purchases, please contact Simon & Schuster Special Sales at 1-866-506-1949 or business@simonandschuster.com.

The Simon & Schuster Speakers Bureau can bring authors to your live event. For more information or to book an event, contact the Simon & Schuster Speakers Bureau at 1-866-248-3049 or visit our website at www.simonspeakers.com.

Manufactured in the United States of America

1 2025

Library of Congress Control Number: 2025947958

ISBN 978-1-5072-2443-4
ISBN 978-1-5072-2444-1 (ebook)

CONTENTS

INTRODUCTION

If you're intimidated or confused by Medicare—the federal government's health insurance program for older Americans and younger people with disabilities—you're not alone. Most Americans become eligible for Medicare at age sixty-five, regardless of their income, health, family situation, or where they live. After qualifying for Medicare, you no longer have to rely on your employer for health insurance or pay high premiums for limited options on the individual health insurance marketplace. Instead, you can get low-cost, comprehensive healthcare coverage from Medicare.

In *Medicare 101*, you'll find simple, easy-to-understand, and up-to-date information that you can personalize to help you make the right decisions for your specific needs. Plus, you'll learn how to avoid costly pitfalls like expensive coverage gaps, late enrollment penalties, and unnecessary costs. You might even find that becoming eligible for Medicare coverage gives you the freedom to retire early, start a business, move to a new area, or use any preferred doctors and hospitals.

Medicare can give you peace of mind about your health coverage as you get older—if you understand how it works. *Medicare 101* will help you navigate this complex system to make the most of its valuable coverage. You'll find clear guidance about how Medicare works, including:

- A full explanation of Medicare's parts, coverage plans, and associated costs
- How to determine whether your prescriptions are covered
- Understanding the pros and cons of Medicare Advantage
- A list of supplemental policies you can purchase to cover the gaps in Medicare
- Step-by-step advice on appealing a claim denial
- Guidance on accessing preventive, chronic conditions, and end-of-life care
- And more

Whether you're signing up for Medicare soon, you've had the coverage for a long time, or you're helping a family member manage their coverage, *Medicare 101* has straightforward answers to all your pressing questions. Having this essential support at your fingertips will give you the confidence you need to make the most of this beneficial program. It's time to understand how Medicare can make big differences in your health and finances, so let's begin.

Chapter 1

Medicare Coverage and Costs

Medicare is the federal government's solution to providing healthcare resources for those sixty-five and older, as well as younger people with certain disabilities. Medicare takes care of most of your medical expenses after you retire, but you must make important decisions about when to sign up, which parts to sign up for, whether to get your coverage from the government program or a private plan, and how to manage the costs. If you make mistakes, you may end up with gaps in your insurance protection, large medical bills, and lifetime late enrollment penalties. Some of the answers can be very personal depending on your insurance preferences, your other coverage, medical conditions, preferred doctors, and cash flow. Before you can make these decisions, you must understand Medicare's components and your options.

In this chapter, you'll learn more about what Medicare is, its history, the program's different parts, and supplemental coverage that can help protect against Medicare's out-of-pocket expenses. After you know what every piece entails and costs, you can put together a Medicare plan that provides what you need at the right time without having to pay too much.

WHAT IS MEDICARE?

Understanding the Basics

Medicare is a government health insurance program that provides valuable healthcare coverage for nearly 69 million Americans ages sixty-five and older, as well as younger people with certain health issues. Thousands of new people sign up every day.

The program covers a large portion of the cost of hospital stays, doctors' services, outpatient care, medical tests, X-rays, emergency care, surgery, skilled nursing care, hospice care, preventive care, and more. Medicare addresses most medically necessary care without coverage limits, protecting against some of the largest financial risks as you age.

The program is split into many sections, each addressing different aspects of insurance. It starts with Medicare Parts A, B, C (Medicare Advantage), and D. Though complex, Medicare's many parts are crucial to understand as you and your loved ones age and depend on it for healthcare coverage. This entry briefly introduces Medicare's many components so that you have a foundational understanding as you read on.

MEDICARE PART A

Starting in alphabetical order, Medicare Part A covers most costs associated with in-hospital stays. This ranges from food to medication to nursing care. Outside of hospital stays, Part A helps pay for skilled nursing facility care, specialized home health care, and hospice care.

Payroll deductions for FICA taxes that you pay with your paycheck finance Medicare Part A. If you (or your spouse) have paid Medicare taxes for at least 10 years, you likely won't be paying a premium. But you do have to pay a hospital deductible ($1,676 per benefit period in 2025) before coverage kicks in. There are also copayments for long-term hospital stays. A much broader picture of costs appears in the Medicare Part A entry later in this chapter.

MEDICARE PART B

Medicare Part B covers doctors' services and outpatient care, which can include preventive care, vaccines, tests, physical therapy, medical equipment, visits with a primary care doctor or specialist, and more.

Part B is financed primarily through monthly premiums ($185 in 2025). Depending on income, high earners pay an extra $74–$443.90 each month in 2025. You pay a deductible and 20% of the cost of most Part B services, which is called a copayment.

Medicare's Growing Population

On July 30, 1965, President Lyndon B. Johnson signed the Medicare program into law. This was after more than twenty years of efforts in Congress to introduce a healthcare program for aging Americans. Medicare services began on July 1, 1966, covering more than 19 million Americans age sixty-five and older at the time. The program now covers 69 million Americans—90% are age sixty-five and older and 10% are younger people with disabilities.

MEDICARE PART C

The Balanced Budget Act of 1997 established Medicare Part C, giving Medicare beneficiaries the choice to get their coverage from a privately managed care program, originally called Medicare+Choice, rather than from Original Medicare. These plans provide coverage through limited provider networks, similar to workplace health maintenance organizations (HMOs) and preferred provider organizations (PPOs). Renamed Medicare Advantage in 2003, these plans must offer at least as much coverage as Original Medicare and most include extra benefits for prescription drugs, dental, vision, and hearing care rather than having to buy separate policies. Currently, about half of the Medicare beneficiaries are enrolled in Medicare Advantage plans.

Most Medicare Advantage plans charge no premiums in addition to the Medicare Part B premiums. The copayments and deductibles can be different than they are for Original Medicare, and there is an annual out-of-pocket spending cap for covered services.

MEDICARE PART D

The introduction of Medicare Part D prescription drug program as part of the 2003 Medicare Modernization Act drastically changed the landscape in insurance. Medicare originally did not include coverage for prescription drugs, but starting in 2006, Medicare beneficiaries could buy a private Medicare Part D prescription drug plan. People now have a choice of many companies, each with different lists of covered drugs and costs. Premiums are partially subsidized by the federal government. The Inflation Reduction Act of 2022 continued to expand the Part D program, allowing Medicare to negotiate directly with drug companies, covering more vaccines without deductibles or copayments and, most significantly, imposing a $2,000 annual out-of-pocket spending cap for covered prescription drugs starting in 2025. The cap, which is adjusted annually for inflation, is $2,100 in 2026.

MEDIGAP

Even after you sign up for Medicare, you may still have to pay hundreds or thousands of dollars out of your pocket for deductibles and copayments. Some people have secondary health insurance coverage from an employer or former employer that can help pay the Part A and Part B deductibles and copayments. If you have secondary health insurance coverage from an employer, retiree plan, or government program such as TRICARE for military retirees, those plans can cover the out-of-pocket costs. But others who have Original Medicare buy a Medigap policy to fill in those monetary gaps. These policies are sold by private insurance companies but must meet federal coverage standards. If you don't have secondary coverage, you may want to get a private Medigap policy. These policies charge a separate premium.

SIGN-UP PROCESSES

Medicare includes several components that provide much needed healthcare coverage, but they also all have varying sign-up processes. Not only do you need to decide whether to sign up for Medicare at sixty-five—as most people aren't enrolled automatically—but you also need to choose how to get your coverage and whether you want to add additional policies to fill in Medicare's gaps. Each of these components can have different deadlines and sign-up rules, which are explained in their respective entries later in this book. Make your decisions carefully to best take advantage of the program and avoid coverage gaps, late enrollment penalties, and unnecessary expenses. Read on to learn more about each specific piece of Medicare and find the right plan(s) for you.

MEDICARE PART A

Coverage and Costs for Hospital Care

In 1965, the first version of Medicare included two parts, and these parts remain the key components of the program today: Part A covers hospitalization and Part B covers doctors' services and outpatient care. This entry focuses on how Part A covers inpatient hospital care, skilled nursing facility care, and other expensive services.

Most people don't pay Part A premiums because they (or their spouse) paid Medicare taxes from their paychecks for at least ten years (or forty quarters). As a result, most people sign up for Part A when they turn sixty-five, even if they are still working and have employer health insurance coverage. Part A can help pay the high cost of inpatient stays in a hospital or skilled nursing facility. Doctors' services and outpatient care are typically covered by Part B, which charges a monthly premium.

FOUNDATIONAL PART A COSTS

Before we get into the types of services covered under Part A, it's important to understand the costs you have to pay to access those services, including premiums, deductibles, and copayments, and how they impact your overall costs.

Part A Premiums

Most people (99% of beneficiaries) don't pay Medicare Part A premiums because they paid Medicare taxes from their paychecks for ten years or more (which is forty quarters of work, but not necessarily consecutively).

However, if you (or your spouse) don't have that many work credits, you may have to pay monthly premiums. These premiums usually change with inflation each year (see the costs section of Medicare.gov). For example, these are the monthly premiums per person in 2025, based on how long they or their spouse paid Medicare taxes:

- 40 or more work quarters: $0
- 30–39 work quarters: $285
- Fewer than 30 work quarters: $518

Part A Deductible

The Part A deductible is the amount you have to pay for each hospital stay before Medicare coverage kicks in; for example, you pay $1,676 per benefit period in 2025. A benefit period begins the day you're admitted to the hospital as an inpatient or a patient in a skilled nursing facility, and it ends when you've been out of the hospital or skilled nursing facility for sixty consecutive days.

PART A COVERAGE TYPES AND COSTS

Medicare Part A covers many of the costs for hospitalization, some home health care, skilled nursing facility care, and hospice care. This section details what expenses are covered by Part A and what you have to pay for each type of care.

Inpatient Hospital Expenses

Part A covers a semiprivate room and meals, nursing care, drugs and medical supplies you use in the hospital, some blood transfusions, and inpatient rehabilitation. After you pay the Part A deductible (which is $1,676 in 2025), Medicare pays the full cost for the first sixty days in the hospital for each benefit period. Once past the sixty-day mark, you have to pay a portion of the costs. Here's an example of what you will have to pay for a hospital stay in 2025:

- First 60 days per benefit period: $0.
- Days 61–90: $419 per day.
- Days 91 and beyond: $838 per day for up to 60 lifetime reserve days (lifetime reserve days can be applied to different benefit periods). You then take on all costs after you use up your lifetime reserve days.

Remember: Even if you qualify for premium-free Part A, you'll still have to pay deductibles and copayments for inpatient stays in a hospital. The new figures for these deductibles and copays are usually announced in October or November for the next calendar year.

Skilled Nursing Facility Care

Part A pays for the first twenty days in a skilled nursing facility providing rehabilitation after at least three days as an inpatient during a hospital stay. It covers skilled nursing care, room and meals, and medical equipment and supplies used in the facility. It can also pay for physical therapy, occupational therapy, speech-language pathology services, and ambulance transportation if needed to receive the services.

To qualify, your physician has to state that you need daily skilled care from nurses or therapists. You will not be covered if you just need help with the activities of daily living (custodial care) rather than skilled nursing or rehab care.

Medicare will cover the first twenty days of eligible care, and you'll have to pay a portion of the cost after that. These amounts change each year—for example, you have to pay the following per benefit period in 2025:

- Days 1–20: $0
- Days 21–100: $209.50 per day
- More than 100 days: You pay all costs

Inpatient versus Observation Care

To qualify for skilled nursing facility care coverage from Medicare, you must have spent at least three days in a hospital receiving inpatient care. You do not qualify if you were only in the hospital under observation. The distinction is important: For example, if you spent one night in the hospital receiving observation services before being admitted as an inpatient for two nights, you will not qualify for skilled nursing coverage since you were considered an outpatient during that one night under observation.

Home Health Care

Part A can cover some part-time skilled care at home for patients who are homebound. The doctor must certify that you need skilled nursing care, physical therapy, occupational therapy, or speech-language pathology. You must receive the care from a Medicare-approved home health agency. Medicare covers most of the cost of certain home health care services if you are eligible, including medically necessary part-time or intermittent skilled nursing care, physical therapy, occupational therapy, speech-language pathology services, and medical social services. Medicare does not pay for care twenty-four hours per day, and it doesn't cover custodial care if that is the only care you need. The home health agency must tell you in advance if any of the services it provides will not be covered.

Hospice Care

Part A covers hospice care for people who are terminally ill if their doctor certifies that they have a life expectancy of six months or less. Once you're placed in hospice, you receive comfort care rather than care to treat your terminal illness. You may have to pay the following hospice costs: up to $5 per prescription for pain and symptom management and 5% of the cost for inpatient respite care to give the caregiver a break.

MEDICARE PART B

Coverage for Doctors, Tests, and Preventive Care

While Medicare Part A covers most of the costs related to staying in a hospital, Medicare Part B covers doctors' services and outpatient care. The wide variety of Part B coverages are detailed throughout the rest of this entry.

PART B COSTS

There are three components of Part B costs: the premium, deductible, and coinsurance, which is the 20% portion of the cost that you pay for most covered services.

Premiums

You pay a monthly premium for Part B, which is $185 per month for most people in 2025. People with high incomes may have to pay more—from $74 to $443.90 extra each month in 2025, depending on how much money they earn. You can find the premiums on the Medicare costs page at Medicare.gov. Costs can change each year and are usually announced in October or November.

Deductible

You pay an annual deductible, which is a dollar amount you pay before most Part B coverage kicks in. The deductible is $257 in 2025. This is similar to a deductible you may have had to pay with an employer health insurance plan.

Coinsurance

This is the percentage of the costs you have to pay yourself. Medicare Part B typically pays 80% of the cost of doctors' services and outpatient care, and you pay 20% of the Medicare-approved amount. However, you can receive some preventive services without having to pay the deductible or coinsurance, such as most vaccines and screenings for several types of cancer and other diseases, depending on your age and risk factors.

How Assignment Affects Doctor's Charges

You typically pay 20% of the doctor's costs covered by Part B. If a doctor "accepts assignment," they agree to charge you no more than the amount Medicare approved for that service. But you may have to pay more if the doctor doesn't accept assignment, meaning the doctor doesn't take what Medicare has approved for their assistance. In that case, the doctor can request up to 15% more than what Medicare has approved—so you'd have to pay up to 15% in addition to the 20%.

Get Help with Part B Costs

If your income is below a certain level, you may qualify for financial assistance from a Medicare Savings Program, which can help pay Medicare Part A and Part B premiums, deductibles, copayments, and coinsurance. See the costs section of Medicare.gov for details.

PART B SERVICES

Part B covers many preventive services without any deductibles or coinsurance charges. They may include:

- Vaccines, such as hepatitis B, flu shots, pneumococcal shots (although some vaccines, such as the shingles vaccine, are covered by Part D prescription drug coverage instead).
- Screenings, such as for cervical and vaginal cancer, colorectal cancer, diabetes, lung cancer, prostate cancer, mammograms, and depression. Coverage is based on your age and risk factors.
- Preventive care and counseling programs, including alcohol counseling, diabetes prevention program, medical nutrition therapy services, obesity behavioral therapy, a "Welcome to Medicare" preventive visit, and a yearly wellness visit.

Though not for free, there are some things you can get for reduced cost when using Medicare. Part B also covers 80% of the cost of doctors' services and outpatient care, including:

- Doctors' visits and medically necessary services from doctors and other healthcare workers.
- Diagnostic tests.
- Some prescription drugs administered in the doctor's office.
- Durable medical equipment that you use in your home (like wheelchairs, scooters, and walkers).
- Ambulance services, when transporting yourself would put you in danger.
- Outpatient physical therapy, occupational therapy, and speech-language pathology services.
- Eligible emergency department visits. (Part A covers the expense if you're admitted to the hospital for a related condition within three days.)

There are so many benefits for Medicare Part B, both free and reduced cost alike, but before you get them, you have to sign up.

WHEN TO SIGN UP FOR PART B

You can sign up for Part B during your initial enrollment period, which is a seven-month period that starts three months before the month you turn sixty-five and ends three months later. If you sign up before your birthday month, your coverage will take effect the first of the month you turn sixty-five (or the beginning of the previous month, if your birthday is on the first). Otherwise, your coverage starts the beginning of the month after you sign up.

If you don't happen to have health insurance through an employer, you usually must sign up for Part B during this initial enrollment period. Otherwise, you may have to wait until the next general enrollment period to sign up, which runs from January 1 to March 31 each year, and you may have to pay a late enrollment penalty for as long as you have Medicare.

If you or your spouse are still working and you have health insurance through an employer with twenty or more employees, then you can delay signing up for Medicare Part B without late penalties or coverage gaps. However, you must sign up within eight months of leaving that job and losing the coverage, or else you may have to pay a late enrollment penalty.

PART B
LATE ENROLLMENT PENALTY

If you miss the sign-up deadlines, you may have to pay a late enrollment penalty. The late penalty adds 10% to the standard Part B premium for each twelve-month period when you should have had

Part B but hadn't enrolled. This late penalty lasts for as long as you have Part B, which is usually for your lifetime.

Medicare History

Medicare has been around for decades. The program has evolved significantly since it was first introduced in 1965, offering additional coverage, options, and costs through the years. Medicare originally included two parts: Part A and Part B. These together are called "Original Medicare" or "traditional Medicare," and they both continue to serve as the core of the Medicare program.

MEDICARE PART C

Medicare Advantage's All-in-One Private Coverage

After you sign up for Medicare Part A and Part B, you have a choice: You can either get your coverage through Original Medicare, the government program that lets you use any doctor who participates, or you can sign up for a private Medicare Advantage plan, an all-in-one plan that has provider networks, different cost sharing (the deductibles, copayments, and coinsurance you pay yourself), and may provide some additional coverage. These plans have been growing in popularity—about half of Medicare beneficiaries are now enrolled in Medicare Advantage plans rather than Original Medicare.

You usually have several Medicare Advantage plans to choose from in your area, with different premiums, cost sharing, drug coverage, and provider networks. In 2026, the average Medicare beneficiary has thirty-two Medicare Advantage plans to choose from that include both medical and drug coverage, according to KFF (a health policy and research organization). You can compare plans available in your area by using the plan finder at Medicare .gov (www.medicare.gov/plan-compare).

WHAT DOES MEDICARE ADVANTAGE COVER?

Medicare Advantage plans must provide at least as much coverage as Medicare Part A and Part B, but they may have different out-of-pocket costs. Most plans also include Part D prescription drug coverage, rather than having to buy a standalone plan, and they tend to provide other benefits that aren't included in Original Medicare, such as some coverage for dental, hearing, and vision care. Some plans may also help pay for transportation to and from doctors' appointments, a flex card to pay for over-the-counter drugs, and a grocery allowance for healthy food (which may be limited to people with chronic conditions).

Medicare Advantage plans tend to have more prior authorization requirements than Original Medicare. This means that your doctor must provide extra documentation explaining why you need the medical treatment, even if it's covered by the plan.

Medicare Advantage Special Needs Plans

Some Medicare Advantage plans provide special coordinated coverage for people in certain situations, called special needs plans (SNPs). These plans may be available for people with certain chronic conditions (C-SNP), people who are enrolled in both Medicare and Medicaid (called dual eligibles, D-SNP) or people who are living in an institutional setting, such as a nursing home (I-SNP). Availability of these special needs plans can vary significantly throughout the country.

What Doctors Can You Use?

One of the biggest differences between Original Medicare and Medicare Advantage is the doctors you can use. Original Medicare lets you use any doctor who participates in the program. Medicare Advantage plans usually have limited provider networks.

Most Medicare Advantage plans are either HMOs or PPOs, similar to employer plans. With an HMO, you choose a primary care doctor, and you usually need a referral to see a specialist. You may not have any coverage for out-of-network providers except in emergencies.

With a PPO, you don't need a referral to see a specialist, but you will have lower copayments and out-of-pocket limits if you use in-network providers. You can usually go to an out-of-network provider, too, but you'll have to pay more.

You must determine whether the doctors you want to use are covered by the plan and your coverage if you go to an out-of-network doctor.

WHAT DOES MEDICARE ADVANTAGE COST?

You must sign up for Medicare Part A and Part B before you can enroll in a Medicare Advantage plan. You have to pay Part B premiums, which are $185 per month in 2025 (some people also have to pay Part A premiums if they didn't pay Medicare taxes for long enough to qualify for premium-free Part A).

Some Medicare Advantage plans also charge a monthly premium (averaging $14 per month in 2026); however, two-thirds of the Medicare Advantage plans with Part D prescription drug coverage don't charge a monthly premium, other than the Part B premium. Yet, other plans also reduce the Part B premium.

Medicare Advantage plans can charge different cost sharing (the deductibles, copayments, and coinsurance you pay yourself) than Original Medicare. Rather than the hospital deductible, which is $1,676 for Medicare Part A in 2025, you may have to pay a daily amount for hospital stays, such as $460 for each of the first five days at an in-network hospital, with $0 for day six and beyond. Instead of the 20% copayment for doctors' services in Part B, you may have to pay, for example, $50 for a doctor's visit with an in-network specialist, $45 for diagnostic tests, and up to $225 for MRIs. The specific copayments vary by plan.

Unlike Original Medicare, Medicare Advantage plans have an out-of-pocket spending limit for medical care, which is $9,250 for in-network services and $13,900 for plans that cover both in-network and out-of-network services in 2026. Plans can have lower limits. This limit applies to covered medical care; it doesn't apply to premiums or prescription drugs.

Medicare Advantage plans that include prescription drug coverage must limit out-of-pocket costs for covered drugs to $2,100 in 2026, just like standalone Part D plans. This number rises each year for inflation.

WHEN CAN YOU SIGN UP FOR MEDICARE ADVANTAGE?

You can sign up for a Medicare Advantage plan during your initial enrollment period when you turn sixty-five, after you enroll in Medicare Part A and Part B. You can also enroll or switch plans each year during open enrollment from October 15 to December 7. If you already have a Medicare Advantage plan, you can also switch to a different plan from January 1 to March 31 each year.

You can switch into a Medicare Advantage plan with a five-star quality rating any time during the year. There is a special enrollment period that lets you switch into a five-star plan one time between December 8 of the year before the plan year and November 30 of the plan year, with the additional week included in the annual open enrollment period. You can type your zip code into the Plan Finder at Medicare.gov to see if there are any five-star plans in your area.

You can also sign up or switch plans midyear in other circumstances—for example, if you move out of the plan's service area or you lose employer coverage. These are all considered special enrollment periods, which you can participate in when certain life events happen.

MEDICARE PART D

Prescription Drug Coverage and Costs

Interestingly, Medicare doesn't automatically cover prescription drugs. In fact, the program didn't offer any outpatient prescription drug coverage for its first forty years. The Medicare Prescription Drug, Improvement, and Modernization Act (MMA) of 2003 introduced the Medicare Part D prescription drug program that took effect in 2006 to help cover these expenses. This voluntary coverage is offered by private insurance companies that are regulated by the federal government.

There are two ways to get Medicare drug coverage. If you have Original Medicare, the government-run program that covers any doctor who participates, you can buy a standalone Part D plan. If you choose Medicare Advantage from a private insurer, which typically has provider networks, Part D drug coverage is usually included in your plan.

You can buy Part D when you first enroll in Medicare or when you lose other drug coverage, and you can switch plans every year during open enrollment from October 15 to December 7 with new coverage starting January 1.

It's important to consider prescription drug coverage when making your Medicare enrollment decisions, even if you don't take many medications now. If you don't sign up for Part D when you first enroll in Medicare and you go sixty-three days or more without comparable drug coverage from another source (such as an employer or a retiree plan), you may have to pay a monthly late enrollment penalty if you sign up later.

You have several Part D plans to choose from, depending on where you live. The average Medicare beneficiary has a choice of eight to twelve standalone Part D plans in 2026, according to KFF. Some insurers offer several plans in a region, each with different coverage and costs.

WHAT DRUGS DOES PART D COVER?

The federal government sets rules for the types of drugs Part D plans must cover, but the plans aren't required to cover all drugs. The plan's list of covered drugs is called a formulary. Part D plan formularies must include all drugs in certain protected classes, including drugs for cancer, HIV/AIDS, antidepressants, antipsychotics, anticonvulsants, and immunosuppressants for organ transplants.

Otherwise, the plan's formulary must include at least two drugs in each of the most commonly prescribed categories. The drugs each plan chooses to cover can vary a lot.

Prescription Drugs Covered by Part B

Prescription drugs administered in a doctor's office are covered by Medicare Part B rather than Part D. For example, chemotherapy drugs are typically covered by Part B. Part D covers the shingles vaccine and a few others, but most vaccines are covered by Part B.

NEW RULES SIMPLIFY
PART D COVERAGE

The federal government sets the framework for Part D coverage. In the past, Part D plans had a patchwork of confusing coverage levels—including the notorious "donut hole" where you had to pay the full cost for your medications after your drug costs reached a certain level.

The donut hole was gradually phased out and completely disappeared in 2025, when the Inflation Reduction Act of 2022 made Part D coverage much easier to understand. Now, all Part D plans must cap out-of-pocket costs for covered drugs when your spending reaches a certain level that can increase each year with inflation. The cap started out at $2,000 per year in 2025 and rose to $2,100 for 2026. You don't pay for the drugs covered by your plan after that point. (Premiums are not included in the $2,100 cap.)

Out-of-pocket costs can include the deductible and cost sharing for your medications.

Deductible

Many plans have a deductible before most coverage kicks in. The maximum deductible changes each year and is announced in the fall; go to Medicare.gov to find current costs. The maximum deductible is $615 in 2026, but some plans have lower deductibles.

Cost Sharing

The plan can charge copayments (a fixed dollar amount) or coinsurance (a percentage of the cost) for your medications. These cost-sharing amounts are the portion of the drug costs you pay yourself.

Part D plans typically have four or five pricing tiers with different cost-sharing amounts. For example, a plan may charge $0 for preferred generic drugs or $5 for a thirty-day supply of other generics. It may charge 20% of the cost of preferred brand-name drugs or 40% coinsurance for non-preferred drugs. Some plans have another pricing tier for specialty medications.

Specifics vary by plan, and each plan can put drugs in different tiers—your medication may be preferred in one plan but non-preferred in another, and some plans may not cover it at all. You can compare how the plans in your area cover your necessary medications at Medicare.gov.

PART D PREMIUMS, SURCHARGES, AND EXTRA HELP

Part D plans are offered by private insurance companies, but, as part of the Medicare program, they are regulated by the Centers for Medicare & Medicaid Services (CMS). Monthly premiums vary by plan, but they must be approved by CMS. Even though the average premium is $34.50 in 2026, some plans charge over $100 per month.

People with high incomes pay a monthly surcharge in addition to the Part D premium, called an Income-Related Monthly Adjustment Amount (IRMAA). There are five tiers of surcharges based on income. The income levels and size of the surcharges typically increase every year. In 2025, single tax filers with modified adjusted gross incomes of more than $106,000 and joint filers earning more than $212,000 pay a Part D surcharge ranging from $13.70 to $85.80 per person each month.

The surcharge is based on your last tax return on file—which is usually two years earlier—but you may be able to get the surcharge reduced if your income has dropped since then because of certain life-changing events, such as retirement, divorce, or death of a spouse.

People with low incomes can get help paying Part D premiums and copayments from the Extra Help program, also known as the Low-Income Subsidy. You can find current eligibility requirements at Medicare.gov.

MEDIGAP

Private Coverage to Supplement Medicare

Even after you enroll in Medicare Part A and Part B, you still have some out-of-pocket costs. Part A has a deductible you must pay before coverage kicks in for hospitalization ($1,676 in 2025). Even though Part A covers the first sixty days of a hospital stay, after that you'll have to pay part of the cost for each day hospitalized from day sixty-one to ninety ($419 in 2025), and you'll pay even more for longer hospital stays.

Part B has an annual deductible ($257 in 2025), and you must pay 20% of the cost of most doctors' services and outpatient care, although preventive services are usually free. If your doctor doesn't accept the Medicare-approved payment (known as "accepting assignment"), you may have to pay more. Original Medicare does not have a maximum out-of-pocket spending limit.

However, there are several ways to help fill in these gaps and limit your out-of-pocket costs. If you have coverage from an employer, health insurance from a former employer as a retiree, TRICARE coverage as a military retiree, or other secondary coverage, it can help pay Medicare's out-of-pocket costs. Otherwise, you may want to consider getting a Medigap policy, also known as Medicare Supplement Insurance.

These policies, which are sold by private insurers for a separate premium, can help pay the deductibles, coinsurance, and some other expenses that aren't covered by Original Medicare, such as foreign travel emergency coverage. These plans supplement Original Medicare; you can't have a Medigap policy if you have a Medicare Advantage plan.

WHAT DOES MEDIGAP COVER?

Private insurers sell Medigap policies, but the coverage is standardized by the federal government. There are currently ten types of Medigap plans in most states, with the coverage designated by letters A, B, C, D, F, G, K, L, M, and N. Every plan with the same letter designation must offer the same coverage, but premiums can vary by insurer. Plans C and F are only available to people who were eligible for Medicare before 2020, even if they didn't sign up for Medigap then.

The Medigap policy supplements Original Medicare coverage, and you can use any doctor or hospital who accepts Medicare. All Medigap plans cover the Part A hospital coinsurance and the 20% Part B coinsurance in full or part. Most Medigap plans cover the Part A hospital deductible in full or partially, and Plans F and G cover the Part B excess charges for doctors who don't accept assignment. Many Medigap plans cover up to 80% of foreign travel emergency coverage, which typically isn't covered by Medicare. See the Medigap section of Medicare.gov for a list of what each plan covers.

If you buy a Medigap policy, you may end up with very few out-of-pocket costs throughout the year. For example, Plan G covers most of Medicare's deductibles and copayments except for the Part B deductible. Some of the plans have high-deductible versions or charge a fixed copay for doctors' visits and emergency room visits, often in return for lower premiums. However, Massachusetts, Minnesota, and Wisconsin have different standardized coverage.

MEDIGAP COSTS

Even though each Medigap policy with the same letter designation must provide the same coverage, insurers can charge different premiums for the coverage—even for the same person in the same area. After you decide which letter policy you want, compare premiums and the way the policies are priced. There are three types of Medigap pricing, which can affect what happens to the premiums each year. Not every option is available in all states. The three types are:

- **Issue age policy:** This policy bases premiums on your age when you first buy the policy. Premiums can increase because of inflation.
- **Attained-age policy:** Under this policy, premiums increase based on your current age and inflation.
- **Community-rated policy:** This policy charges the same premium to everyone with the same policy regardless of age.

Many state insurance department websites have a list of each Medigap insurer's premiums for each type of policy available in your area by age.

However, your premiums may be higher if you didn't buy a policy within a certain time frame and you have preexisting conditions. See the following sections for more information about those rules.

WHEN IS THE BEST TIME TO GET MEDIGAP COVERAGE?

Medigap isn't required, but it can help cover potentially open-ended out-of-pocket costs if you have Original Medicare.

You can technically get a Medigap policy at any time after you sign up for Medicare Part A and Part B. But if you don't buy it at certain times, Medigap insurers in most states can reject you or charge more because of preexisting conditions—which is not the case with other types of Medicare coverage. However, there are certain time frames and situations when Medigap insurers must offer you coverage regardless of your health, called guaranteed issue rights.

Medigap Open Enrollment Period

If you sign up for Medigap within six months of enrolling in Medicare Part B at age sixty-five or older, insurers have to offer you any policy available in the state, regardless of your health. As long as you continue to pay premiums, you may keep your policy. The rules may be different for people who qualify for Medicare before sixty-five because of a disability.

Other Guaranteed Issue Rights

After those six months, insurers must also offer you certain Medigap policies regardless of preexisting conditions in special situations. Examples of these guaranteed issue rights include: if you have Original Medicare and you lose employer coverage that was secondary to Medicare (such as coverage from an employer with fewer than twenty employees, retiree coverage, or COBRA continuation coverage); you have a Medicare Advantage plan and you move out of the plan's service area; or you decide to leave a Medicare Advantage plan within the first year and switch to Original Medicare.

States with Special Rules

You can buy a Medigap policy at any time regardless of preexisting conditions in a few states, including Connecticut, Massachusetts, and New York.

Some states, such as Virginia and California, let you switch plans regardless of preexisting conditions at certain times of the year, such as sixty days after your birthday each year. However, this guaranteed issue right may be limited to people who already have Medigap plans and are moving into another plan with the same or lesser benefits.

Medigap Premiums with Preexisting Conditions

If you don't qualify for guaranteed issue rights, insurers in most states can reject you for coverage or charge more for Medigap policies because of preexisting conditions. The types of medical conditions and the impact on your rates can vary a lot by insurer.

THE INCOME-RELATED MONTHLY ADJUSTMENT AMOUNT (IRMAA)

Who Pays and How Do You Reduce It?

If your income is above a certain level, you may have to pay more for your Medicare Part B and Part D premiums. This high-income surcharge, called the Income-Related Monthly Adjustment Amount (IRMAA), was first added to Part B premiums in 2007, and then added to Part D prescription drug premiums in 2011. About 8% of Medicare beneficiaries with Part B or Part D must pay this monthly surcharge in addition to their regular premiums.

There are five tiers of IRMAA surcharges based on your modified adjusted gross income. Your modified adjusted gross income is your AGI (line 11 of IRS Form 1040) plus tax-exempt interest income (line 2a of Form 1040), which includes tax-exempt interest from municipal bonds. The size of the surcharges and the income levels they apply to usually increase each year. Go to Medicare.gov and type in "Medicare costs" for Part B and Part D surcharge amounts.

In 2025, the surcharge applies to single tax filers with modified adjusted gross incomes above $106,000 and joint filers earning more than $212,000.

High earners who have Part D prescription drug coverage (either from a standalone plan or through Medicare Advantage), also have to pay a monthly surcharge on top of their regular Part D premiums. Part D premiums are paid to the plan, but the surcharge is paid to Medicare.

The following chart shows the income tiers and corresponding surcharges for 2025.

MONTHLY MEDICARE HIGH-INCOME SURCHARGES FOR 2025

SINGLE FILER INCOME	JOINT FILER INCOME	PART B SURCHARGE	PART D SURCHARGE
$106,000 or less	$212,000 or less	$0	$0
$106,001–$133,000	$212,001–$266,000	$74.00	$13.70
$133,001–$167,000	$266,001–$334,000	$185.00	$35.30
$167,001–$200,000	$334,001–$400,000	$295.90	$57.00
$200,001–$499,999	$400,001–$749,999	$406.90	$78.60
$500,000 or more	$750,000 or more	$443.90	$85.80

HOW TO GET THE SURCHARGE REDUCED OR ELIMINATED

You may be able to get the surcharge reduced or eliminated if your income has recently dropped for certain reasons. The surcharge is based on your modified adjusted gross income from your last income tax return on file. That is typically the return from two years ago. However, if your income has dropped since then because of certain life-changing events, you can ask the Social Security Administration to base your premiums on your newer, lower income level.

You can only qualify to get the surcharge reduced if your income changed for one of the following reasons:

- Marriage
- Divorce/annulment
- Death of your spouse

- Work stoppage or reduction
- Loss of income-producing property
- Loss of pension income
- Employer settlement payment

If you qualify, the Social Security Administration can use your more recent income to determine whether you have to pay the surcharge. To request the reduction, submit Form SSA-44 to the Social Security Administration (go to www.ssa.gov and type "request to lower an IRMAA" into the search bar). You'll need to provide evidence of the life-changing event. Note that it may take time for the Social Security Administration to process the paperwork, and you may need to pay the surcharge while you wait, but you'll get back the extra amount you paid retroactively if the reduction is approved.

WHO CAN'T GET THE SURCHARGE REDUCED

You can only get the surcharge reduced if you experienced one of the eligible life-changing events. You can't get the amount changed if your income was unusually high in that year for other reasons. In that case, you'll have to pay the surcharge for a year. That said, the surcharges are calculated every year, and your premiums may be lower for the following year if your income has dropped.

If your income is close to the cutoff for the surcharge, be careful about making moves that could boost your income, such as taking large withdrawals from tax-deferred retirement accounts or converting a lot of money from a traditional IRA to a Roth.

Chapter 2

Medicare Enrollment Decisions

You can enroll in Medicare at sixty-five, but the steps aren't the same for everyone. You have several options to create a comprehensive plan. The best solutions can vary by person and circumstances, but the process always has the same five decisions:

- When to enroll in Part A (premium-free for most people)
- When to enroll in Part B (includes a monthly premium)
- Whether to choose Original Medicare (the government program where you can use any doctor) or a private Medicare Advantage plan (which has a limited provider network but may have additional coverage)
- Whether you'd like to supplement Original Medicare with a private Medigap policy to help pay for out-of-pocket costs
- When to get separate Part D prescription drug coverage

A key factor in your Medicare decisions is if you or your spouse are still working. If you have health insurance from a current employer, you may not need to sign up for Medicare or get any supplemental policies at sixty-five. But if you're retired, you usually need to sign up during the seven-month initial enrollment period surrounding your sixty-fifth birthday. Regardless of your situation, you'll need to meet key deadlines to avoid coverage gaps and late penalties. This chapter will explore how to make the best choices for your personal situation.

MEDICARE FOR THE UNEMPLOYED

Enroll at Sixty-Five Without Employer Coverage

If you and your spouse are both retired and you don't have health insurance from a current employer, you almost always need to sign up for Medicare Part A and Part B at age sixty-five. Even if you have other coverage—such as from a retiree health insurance plan, COBRA continuation coverage from an employer plan, or TRICARE for military retirees—that coverage becomes secondary to Medicare once you turn sixty-five. You could end up with big coverage gaps and a late enrollment penalty if you don't sign up.

Primary versus Secondary Coverage

You may have more than one type of health insurance after you turn sixty-five and become eligible for Medicare. The primary coverage is the policy that pays first. Secondary coverage can help pay costs that aren't covered by the primary policy, such as deductibles and copayments.

DECISIONS FOR PEOPLE NOT WORKING AT SIXTY-FIVE

There are a few key decisions to make at sixty-five if you and your spouse aren't working. This section goes through them.

Sign Up for Medicare During Your Initial Enrollment Period

Unless you qualify earlier because of a disability, the first time you can sign up for Medicare is during your initial enrollment period, which begins three months before the month you turn sixty-five and lasts for three months after your birth month. If you sign up before your birth month, your Medicare coverage will take effect the first of the month you turn sixty-five (or the first of the previous month if your birthday is on the first).

If you sign up during your birth month or the three months afterward, your Part B coverage will take effect the first of the following month. You can sign up for premium-free Part A at any time, and your coverage will take effect six months retroactively, but no earlier than the month you turn sixty-five.

If You Miss the Initial Enrollment Period

If you don't have health insurance from a current employer and you don't sign up for Medicare during your initial enrollment period, then you may end up with some of the following negative consequences.

Coverage Gaps

Medicare generally becomes your primary coverage at sixty-five, and any other coverage may not pay out if you don't sign up for Medicare at sixty-five. So, you may end up with large gaps in your coverage.

Limited Opportunities to Sign Up

If you don't sign up for Medicare before your initial enrollment period is over, then you may have to wait until the general enrollment period from January 1 to March 31 to sign up for Part B. (You can enroll in Part A any time after you turn sixty-five if you qualify for premium-free coverage.)

Late Penalties

If you don't have health insurance from a current employer and you don't sign up for Part B during your initial enrollment period, you may have to pay a late enrollment penalty. This penalty adds 10% to the standard Part B premium for each twelve-month period when you should have had Part B. It lasts as long as you have the coverage, which is usually your lifetime.

Special Rules for Federal Retirees

Retiree coverage is usually secondary to Medicare when you turn sixty-five, but there is one exception: Federal retiree coverage can remain your primary coverage. You don't have to sign up for Medicare, and your policy will continue to pay out first. However, if you change your mind and enroll in Medicare later, you may have to pay a late enrollment penalty. Make sure to compare the coverage and costs before deciding.

OTHER DECISIONS AFTER YOU ENROLL IN MEDICARE

Medicare Part A and Part B may not cover all your medical expenses. After you enroll in Medicare, you'll need to take additional steps to make sure you have all the coverage you need.

Choose Between Original Medicare or Medicare Advantage

After you sign up for Medicare Part A and Part B, you need to decide whether you want your coverage from Original Medicare, the government-run program that covers any doctor who participates, or from a private Medicare Advantage plan, which usually has provider networks but additional coverage. Your next steps will depend on that choice.

If You Choose Original Medicare

You'll have two other decisions to make if you choose Original Medicare: Do you need a Medigap policy and a Part D prescription drug plan?

Do You Need Medigap?

Medicare has deductibles, copayments, and other out-of-pocket costs. If you have other health insurance, such as a retiree health insurance plan or TRICARE for Life for military retirees, that may help cover those expenses. Otherwise, you may want to buy a Medigap policy from a private insurer.

The best time to sign up is within six months after enrolling in Medicare Part B at sixty-five or older, when Medigap insurers must offer the policy at the best price for your age and gender. Once past the six-month mark, Medigap insurers in most states can reject you for coverage or charge more because of preexisting conditions.

Do You Need Part D Prescription Drug Coverage?

Original Medicare doesn't automatically cover prescription drugs, but you can buy Part D prescription drug coverage to help with those costs. You may not need to buy Part D if you have similar drug coverage from another source, such as retiree coverage. But if you go for sixty-three days or more without drug coverage that is at least as good as Part D, called "creditable coverage," then you may have to pay a late enrollment penalty. This penalty adds 1% of the national base beneficiary Part D premium ($38.99 per month in 2026) times the number of months you went without creditable coverage since enrolling in Part A or Part B. The monthly penalty lasts as long as you have Medicare drug coverage. (The base beneficiary premium is different from the average premium.)

If you don't sign up for Part D during your initial enrollment period, you may also have limited opportunities to sign up. You can get Part D during the annual open enrollment period from October 15 to December 7 for coverage starting January 1. You may also qualify for a special enrollment period in certain situations, such as within two months after losing other drug coverage.

If You Choose Medicare Advantage

If you decide to get coverage from a private Medicare Advantage plan rather than Original Medicare, you'll usually have medical and drug coverage in one plan. You can sign up during your initial enrollment period, or you can get a plan during open enrollment from October 15 to December 7 for coverage starting January 1.

MEDICARE DECISIONS FOR THE EMPLOYED

Delaying Enrollment and Other Options

If you or your spouse are still working at age sixty-five and you have health insurance through a current employer, you may not have to sign up for Medicare right away. The decision depends on the size of your employer.

HEALTH INSURANCE FROM A LARGE EMPLOYER

You can keep your current coverage and sign up for Medicare later. Health insurance from a current employer with twenty or more employees can continue to be your primary coverage after you turn sixty-five, so you won't have coverage gaps if you don't sign up for Medicare. You won't have a late enrollment penalty as long as you sign up for Medicare Part B within eight months of leaving the job and losing that coverage.

Should You Sign Up for Part A?

Many people with employer health insurance still sign up for Part A at sixty-five because they don't have to pay premiums for it. You can sign up for Part A during your initial enrollment period, which starts three months before the month you turn sixty-five and lasts for three months afterward. If you qualify for premium-free

Part A, you can sign up any time without a late enrollment penalty. Coverage will begin up to six months retroactively, but no earlier than the month you turn sixty-five.

However, you may not want to sign up for Part A at sixty-five if you want to contribute to a health savings account (HSA). You can't contribute to an HSA after you sign up for either Medicare Part A or Part B. An HSA is a tax-advantaged way to pay out-of-pocket medical expenses.

You can't delay signing up for Part A if you're already receiving Social Security benefits at least four months before your sixty-fifth birthday; in that case, you will be enrolled in Part A automatically. (People who are already receiving Social Security benefits are automatically enrolled in Part B, too, but you have the option to return your Medicare card and have it reissued for Part A only; you don't have the option to delay Part A if you're already receiving Social Security benefits.)

Should You Sign Up for Part B?

Most people who have health insurance from a large employer choose not to sign up for Part B so they don't have to pay monthly premiums for both Medicare and their employer's plan. If you or your spouse are working, your income could also make you subject to the Medicare high-income surcharge, which could boost your premiums even more.

Heath insurance coverage from a large employer can remain primary, even after you turn sixty-five, and you won't have to pay a late enrollment penalty as long as you sign up within eight months of leaving that job and losing that coverage.

Medicare Advantage, Part D, and Medigap

As long as you have employer coverage, you may not need to make these decisions yet. If you don't sign up for Part B, you can't sign up for Medicare Advantage or Medigap. You may not need Part D as long as you have similar drug coverage from your employer or another source.

HEALTH INSURANCE FROM A SMALL COMPANY

Your decisions are different if your coverage is from an employer with fewer than twenty employees. In that case, you usually have to sign up for Medicare Part A and Part B during your initial enrollment period at age sixty-five. That's because coverage from a small employer usually is secondary to Medicare. (Some small employers have different rules, but that is rare. Check with your HR department.)

If your employer's coverage becomes secondary to Medicare at sixty-five and you don't sign up during your initial enrollment period, you could have coverage gaps and your employer's plan may not pay out. However, since you have some coverage from an active employer, you won't have to pay a late enrollment penalty as long as you sign up for Medicare within eight months of leaving the job and losing that coverage. The rules for avoiding late enrollment penalties apply to employer coverage of any size.

Medigap, Part D, and Medicare Advantage

If you have employer coverage to supplement Medicare, you probably don't need to sign up for Medigap, Part D, or Medicare

Advantage yet. But be careful with the timelines after you leave your job.

Part D Prescription Drug Coverage

You usually need to sign up for a standalone Part D policy or a Medicare Advantage plan with drug coverage within two months of losing the other creditable coverage, which can include drug coverage from an employer plan. If you don't sign up for Medicare prescription drug coverage during this special enrollment period, you may have to wait until open enrollment from October 15 to December 7 for Part D or Medicare Advantage coverage starting January 1. You may have to pay a late enrollment penalty, which adds 1% of the national base beneficiary Part D premium ($38.99 per month in 2026) times the number of months you went without creditable coverage since enrolling in Part A or Part B. The monthly penalty lasts as long as you have Medicare drug coverage.

Medigap

Your employer's health insurance can supplement Medicare while you're working, but you may want to get a Medigap policy after you leave your job, if you don't have any other supplemental coverage.

If you buy a Medigap policy within six months of signing up for Part B at sixty-five or older, Medigap insurers can't charge more or reject you because of preexisting conditions. But if you work for a small employer, you probably didn't need Medigap when you enrolled in Part B. In this case, there is a special rule: If you have other coverage that is secondary to Medicare—from a small employer, retiree coverage, or COBRA continuation coverage—you have up to sixty-three days after losing that coverage to get certain Medigap policies regardless of preexisting conditions.

Medicare Advantage When Still Working

You may not need Medicare Advantage while you have employer coverage, but you may want to get it after you leave your job. You have a two-month special enrollment period to get Medicare Advantage after your employer coverage ends or you can sign up during the annual open enrollment period. You must enroll in Medicare Part A and Part B before you can sign up for Medicare Advantage.

HOW OTHER INSURANCE IMPACTS MEDICARE

Most Coverage Becomes Secondary at Sixty-Five

Some people have other kinds of insurance when they turn sixty-five and become eligible for Medicare. The type of coverage you have determines whether or not you need to sign up for Medicare at sixty-five and what happens to your other coverage.

You generally need to sign up for Medicare at sixty-five unless you or your spouse are still working *and* you have health insurance from an employer with twenty or more employees. In this case, your employer coverage can remain your primary coverage even after sixty-five. However, in most other cases, your other coverage becomes secondary at sixty-five, and you must sign up for Medicare or else you may end up with coverage gaps and late penalties. Secondary coverage pays after Medicare, and if you don't sign up for Medicare, the other policy may not pay out at all.

Medicare works in different ways with other kinds of insurance, which will affect the decisions you make when you turn sixty-five.

HOW MEDICARE WORKS WITH EMPLOYER COVERAGE

If you or your spouse are still working and you have health insurance from a current employer, you can delay signing up for Medicare while you're working and you won't have to pay a late enrollment penalty. However, the way the coverage works with Medicare depends on the size of the employer.

Employers with Twenty or More Employees

Coverage from a large employer is primary and you don't have to sign up for Medicare while you or your spouse are still working. You won't have a late enrollment penalty as long as you sign up for Medicare within eight months of leaving the job and losing the coverage.

Employers with Fewer Than Twenty Employees

Coverage from a small employer is generally secondary to Medicare at sixty-five. You may have coverage gaps or no coverage from the employer plan if you don't sign up for Medicare at sixty-five. There are some exceptions—some employers keep their coverage as primary even after you turn sixty-five. Ask your employer about the rules before making any immediate decisions.

RETIREE COVERAGE

Retiree coverage is almost always secondary to Medicare. You'll need to sign up for Medicare at sixty-five or else you could have coverage gaps and a late penalty.

However, there is one exception: federal employees' retiree coverage. Retiree coverage from the Federal Employees Health Benefits (FEHB) program can remain primary if you don't sign up for Medicare at sixty-five, which means you wouldn't have coverage gaps if you don't sign up. But you will have to pay a Part B late enrollment penalty if you change your mind and decide to sign up for Medicare more than eight months after you leave your job. The US Office of Personnel Management recommends signing up for Part A at sixty-five if you're eligible for premium-free coverage, and deciding whether or not to sign up for Part B based on how the coverage and costs compare to your federal retiree coverage. FEHB drug coverage is considered to be creditable coverage, so you may not need to sign up for Part D.

Medicare and COBRA Continuation Coverage

COBRA is a federal law that requires employers with twenty or more employees to let you continue your health insurance coverage for up to eighteen months after you leave your job. However, when you stop working, the coverage becomes secondary to Medicare. If you have COBRA coverage at sixty-five, you still have to sign up for Medicare or you could have coverage gaps and a late enrollment penalty.

TRICARE MILITARY HEALTHCARE COVERAGE

TRICARE coverage is secondary to Medicare for military retirees. You need to sign up for Medicare Part A and Part B at sixty-five in order to keep your TRICARE coverage. At that point it becomes TRICARE for Life and supplements Medicare, helping to fill in deductibles and copayments and providing some additional coverage, such as for foreign travel emergencies. If you have TRICARE for Life, you usually don't need a Medigap policy or Part D.

VA HEALTH CARE

This healthcare program for veterans, offered through the US Department of Veterans Affairs, is available to a broader group of veterans than TRICARE. You do not need to retire from the military to qualify; instead, you generally need to have served for at least two years (or fewer if discharged for certain disabilities) and not received a dishonorable discharge.

VA Health Care for military veterans is a different system from Medicare. You can continue to go to VA hospitals and use VA providers, if eligible, whether or not you enroll in Medicare. But the US Department of Veterans Affairs recommends that you sign up for Medicare at sixty-five (unless you have employer coverage) so you'll have coverage if you want to use a non-VA provider or facility. If you have VA Health Care and you don't sign up for Medicare at sixty-five (and you don't have employer coverage), you could pay a late enrollment penalty if you change your mind and enroll later.

ACA MARKETPLACE HEALTHCARE

If you have health insurance from an Affordable Care Act (ACA) marketplace, you usually need to sign up for Medicare at sixty-five. You aren't required to drop the ACA policy at sixty-five, but at that point you can no longer qualify for a premium subsidy (a tax credit that helps lower the cost of your monthly premiums for those who are eligible), and the ACA coverage may become more expensive than Medicare. You can't get a new ACA marketplace policy after you're enrolled in Medicare.

The rules are different if you don't qualify for premium-free Part A. In that case, you can keep your ACA marketplace policy, and you may continue to qualify for premium subsidies if you don't enroll in Medicare. But you may have to pay a late enrollment penalty for both Part A and Part B if you decide to enroll in Medicare later.

MEDICAID

If you already qualify for Medicaid, the healthcare program for certain people with low incomes, you can also sign up for Medicare at sixty-five; this is called being "dually eligible." Medicare will pay your bills first and Medicaid may help pay your Medicare premiums, deductibles, and copayments. Medicaid may also pay for some expenses Medicare doesn't cover, such as nursing home costs and dental care in some states. You'll automatically get assistance with prescription drug costs via the Extra Help program; Medicaid may also pay for other drugs that Medicare doesn't cover.

ORIGINAL MEDICARE VERSUS MEDICARE ADVANTAGE

Government Program or Private Plan?

After you enroll in Medicare Part A and Part B, you must make a big decision: Do you want to get coverage from the federal government's Original Medicare program, or do you want to enroll in a private Medicare Advantage plan?

Currently, about half of the Medicare beneficiaries are enrolled in Medicare Advantage plans. There are key differences between the two options, including which doctors you can use, how much you pay out of pocket, if prior authorization restrictions are common, and whether you can get extra coverage for prescription drugs, dental, vision, and hearing care all in one plan.

Read on to learn more about the key features of each type of plan.

ORIGINAL MEDICARE

As previously mentioned, Original Medicare consists of Parts A and B. Under Original Medicare, you can use any doctor throughout the country who participates in the plan, but you may need to buy a few different policies—and pay extra premiums—to cover most out-of-pocket costs. Here are some of the additional factors relating to the original program:

- The vast majority of doctors and other medical providers participate in the Medicare program.
- You don't need permission from a primary care doctor to see a specialist.
- You have coverage throughout the United States.
- You have to pay deductibles and copayments, and there isn't an annual cap on out-of-pocket medical expenses.
- You may need to buy two additional policies with extra premiums to supplement your coverage, including a separate Part D plan for prescription drug coverage and a Medigap plan to fill in coverage gaps.
- If you do get a Medigap plan, you'll have extra premiums but the plan can cover most of your out-of-pocket expenses other than the Part B deductible, which is $257 in 2025.
- Original Medicare doesn't include coverage for dental, vision, or hearing care, except in rare circumstances.
- You rarely need to take extra steps before Original Medicare will cover a service your doctor prescribes; however, there are three situations where you may need to get prior authorization before Medicare will cover the services: nonemergency ambulance services, certain kinds of durable medical equipment, and some dermatology services that could otherwise be considered cosmetic. In these cases, your doctor may need to prove that the services are medically necessary before Medicare will cover them. (A pilot program in six states is testing adding some additional prior authorization requirements for Original Medicare in 2026.)

Original Medicare and Medicare Advantage each have their own strengths; the next section shows Medicare Advantage's.

MEDICARE ADVANTAGE

These all-in-one plans have limited provider networks and may have more prior authorization requirements. However, you may have additional coverage for prescription drugs, dental, vision, and hearing care without paying separate premiums for extra policies. Here are some additional factors:

- You have a limited provider network and may have to pay more to go to an out-of-network provider (typically for PPOs), or you may not have any coverage for out-of-network providers except for emergencies (typically for HMOs).
- You may have limited coverage if you travel outside of your plan's service area.
- Most Advantage plans include coverage for medical care and prescription drugs in one plan.
- Most plans may provide additional coverage, like transportation to doctors' appointments and healthy meals.
- Medicare Advantage special needs plans (SNPs) may provide special coordinated coverage for chronic conditions (C-SNP) or for people who are dually eligible for both Medicare and Medicaid (D-SNP) or for people who living in an institutional setting, like a nursing home (I-SNP).
- Many Medicare Advantage plans have a $0 monthly premium in addition to the Part B premiums. The average Medicare Advantage premium is $14 per month in 2026.
- Medicare Advantage plans must cover at least the same services as Original Medicare, but you may have different out-of-pocket costs.

- Medicare Advantage plans have an out-of-pocket spending cap for medical coverage, which can be no greater than $9,250 for in-network coverage in 2026, and $13,900 for plans that have in-network and out-of-network coverage. This does not include premiums and prescription drug costs. Many Medicare Advantage plans have lower spending caps. (Medicare Advantage plans with prescription drugs also have the same $2,100 out-of-pocket spending cap in 2026 as standalone Part D plans.)
- Medicare Advantage plans tend to require prior authorization before covering more services, which means that your doctor may need to submit extra paperwork to show why you need a service or medication, even if it is covered by the plan.

Difficult to Change Back to Original Medicare

Even though you can switch from Medicare Advantage to Original Medicare during open enrollment, you may have a difficult time getting a Medigap policy. If you leave an Advantage plan more than twelve months after you first sign up for Medicare Advantage, Medigap insurers in most states can reject you for coverage or charge more because of preexisting conditions. So, think carefully.

HOW TO COMPARE COSTS

If you buy Original Medicare plus a Medigap plan, you may have higher premiums but lower out-of-pocket costs throughout the year. However, you may need to pay extra for prescription drugs, dental, vision, and hearing care. Here are the costs you can expect to pay with Original Medicare versus a Medicare Advantage plan:

Costs for Original Medicare

- Part A premium: $0 if you or your spouse paid Medicare taxes for at least ten years
- Part B premium: $185 per month in 2025 (high earners pay more)
- Medigap policy (if purchased): Varies a lot by company, plan, and state; national average for Plan G is about $164 per month
- Part D premiums: Average $34.50 per month in 2026
- Other costs:
  - Part B deductible ($257 in 2025 if you have Original Medicare with Medigap)
  - Part D deductibles and copayments (out-of-pocket costs have a $2,100 cap for 2026)
  - Additional premiums for dental, vision, and hearing care (separate policies must be purchased)

Costs for Medicare Advantage

- Part A premium: $0 if you or your spouse paid Medicare taxes for at least ten years
- Part B premium: $185 per month in 2025 (high earners pay more)
- Medicare Advantage premiums: Average $14 per month in 2026 (but two-thirds of plans have $0 monthly premiums)
- Medical expenses:
  - Maximum out-of-pocket costs for in-network services: $9,250 in 2026

- Maximum out-of-pocket costs for in-network and out-of-network services: $13,900 in 2026
- Prescription drugs:
  - No separate premium for prescription drug coverage
  - Out-of-pocket costs for covered drugs capped at $2,100 in 2026

After you estimate the costs for your current medical expenses, also consider how much it might cost you if you end up having expensive medical needs. That can help put both options into perspective.

ENROLLMENT DEADLINES AND LATE PENALTIES

Avoid Extra Fees and Coverage Gaps

There's a lot at stake when making Medicare enrollment decisions. Not only will you have coverage gaps if you don't sign up at the right time, but you could have to pay late enrollment penalties that last for your lifetime.

This entry outlines when you have to sign up for each type of Medicare, what happens if you miss the deadline, and the penalties for making mistakes.

PART A

You can choose to sign up for Part A during your initial enrollment period, starting three months before the month you turn sixty-five and ending three months later. If you don't have to pay premiums for Part A, you can sign up for Medicare Part A at any time after you turn sixty-five. Your coverage will begin up to six months retroactively, but not before you turn sixty-five. Premiums for Part A are not usually a cause of concern, as most people (or their spouse) have already paid Medicare taxes by working for ten-plus years.

If you have to pay premiums for Part A, then you need to sign up during your initial enrollment period if you and your spouse aren't working, or within eight months of leaving your job and losing employer coverage.

Late Enrollment Penalty

If you have to pay premiums for Part A and you didn't sign up by the deadlines, you may have to pay a late enrollment penalty that increases your monthly premiums by 10%. You'll need to pay this penalty for twice the number of years that you should have signed up for Part A but didn't. There are a few exceptions, such as if you were living outside of the country. If you don't have to pay premiums for Part A, there are no late enrollment penalties.

PART B

You can enroll in Medicare Part B during your seven-month initial enrollment period. If you or your spouse are working and you have health insurance from a current employer, you can sign up for Part B while you have employer coverage or up to eight months after you or your spouse leave the job and lose employer coverage, whichever comes first. If you miss those deadlines, you'll have to wait until the general enrollment period to sign up, which is January 1 to March 31 each year.

Late Enrollment Penalty

If you miss the sign-up deadlines, you may have a late enrollment penalty that adds 10% to the standard Part B premium for each twelve-month period when you should have had Part B but didn't. This penalty lasts as long as you have Part B—usually for the rest of your lifetime.

Avoid the COBRA Trap

A federal law called COBRA requires companies with twenty or more employees to let workers keep their group health insurance coverage for up to eighteen months after they leave their jobs. But even though this coverage looks the same as it did when you were working, it doesn't count as coverage from an active employer. You still have to sign up for Medicare within eight months of leaving the job or losing that coverage, whichever comes first, or else you may have a late enrollment penalty.

PART D PRESCRIPTION DRUG COVERAGE

You can sign up for Part D after you enroll in Part A or Part B during your initial enrollment period, or during the annual open enrollment period from October 15 to December 7 for coverage starting January 1. You can also sign up during a special enrollment period, for example, within two months of losing similar creditable coverage from another source, such as employer, retiree, or COBRA coverage, or in other circumstances, such as moving out of the plan's service area.

Late Enrollment Penalty

If you go sixty-three days or more without creditable drug coverage after your initial enrollment period, you may have a Part D late enrollment penalty, which adds 1% of the national base beneficiary Part D premium (which changes each year; it's $34.50 per month in 2026) times the number of months you went without creditable coverage since enrolling in Part A or Part B. The monthly penalty lasts as long as you have Medicare drug coverage.

MEDICARE ADVANTAGE

You can sign up for a Medicare Advantage plan during your initial enrollment period after enrolling in Medicare Part A and Part B. You can qualify for a two-month special enrollment period in several situations, such as leaving your job and losing your employer coverage, or if you move out of the Medicare Advantage plan's service area. You can also sign up each year during the open enrollment from October 15 to December 7 for coverage starting January 1.

Late Enrollment Penalty

There is no late penalty for Medicare Advantage—you'll just continue to have Original Medicare. However, you may have a Part D late enrollment penalty if you go sixty-three days or more without creditable drug coverage from Medicare Advantage or a standalone Part D plan or another source.

MEDIGAP

You can technically get a Medigap plan any time after you enroll in Medicare Part A and Part B. If you sign up within six months of enrolling in Part B at age sixty-five or later, then you can buy any policy available in your state regardless of preexisting conditions. You can also qualify for guaranteed issue rights—which means insurers must offer you at least some Medigap policies regardless of preexisting conditions—in several other circumstances, such as within sixty-three days of losing secondary coverage from a small employer or retiree plan or if you move out of a Medicare Advantage plan's service area or change your mind within twelve months of enrolling in a Medicare Advantage plan. Some states have special guaranteed issue periods; for example, some let you switch to another Medigap plan with similar benefits during your birthday month.

Late Enrollment Penalty

There is no late enrollment penalty for Medigap, but insurers in most states can charge you more or reject you for coverage because of preexisting conditions unless you buy the policy at certain times.

HOW HSAS IMPACT MEDICARE

Make the Most of Tax-Advantaged Savings

A health savings account (HSA) provides a triple tax break for people who have high-deductible health insurance policies, either through their employers or on their own. Their contributions are tax-deductible (or pre-tax if through their employer), the money grows in the account tax-deferred, and then it can be used tax-free for eligible medical expenses at any time in the future. To be eligible for HSA contributions in 2026, you must have an eligible health insurance policy with a deductible of at least $1,700 if you have self-only health insurance coverage or $3,400 for a family plan.

But you must stop contributing to an HSA when you enroll in Medicare Part A or Part B. Some people who have health insurance from a large employer delay signing up for Medicare Part A, even though they qualify for premium-free coverage, so they can continue to contribute to an HSA.

No Option to Delay Part A If Receiving Social Security

You cannot delay signing up for Part A if you're receiving Social Security benefits at least four months before you turn sixty-five. In that case, you're enrolled automatically in both Part A and Part B. You can send your card back and delay Part B enrollment, but you *must* keep Part A.

However, delaying isn't an option for people who don't have coverage from a large employer. Remember that if you and your spouse aren't working or you have health insurance from an employer with fewer than twenty employees, Medicare may become your primary coverage at sixty-five and you may have coverage gaps (or no coverage) if you don't sign up for Part A and Part B during your initial enrollment period.

STOPPING HSA CONTRIBUTIONS WHEN YOU ENROLL IN MEDICARE

If you decide to delay signing up for Medicare so you can contribute to an HSA, you need to be careful about when you stop contributing. If you sign up for Part A after you turn sixty-five, your Part A coverage will take effect up to six months retroactively, but no earlier than the month you turn sixty-five (or the first of the previous month if your birthday is on the first of the month).

So, you need to stop contributing to your HSA up to six months before you enroll in Medicare Part A. If you're only eligible to contribute to an HSA for part of the year, then your contributions are prorated based on the portion of the year when you were eligible.

In 2026, for example, you can contribute up to $4,400 to an HSA if you're eligible for the full year and have self-only coverage or $8,750 for family coverage. If you're fifty-five or older and not yet enrolled in Medicare, you can contribute an additional $1,000 as a "catch-up" contribution. That means if you're fifty-five or older, you can contribute up to $450 for each month if you had an eligible self-only health insurance policy, or $812.50 for family coverage. If you're older than sixty-five and you plan to enroll in Medicare Part A in September, that means you can only make three months' worth of contributions for the year because of the retroactive Part A coverage.

MEDICARE-RELATED HSA EXPENSES

Even though you can't make new contributions to an HSA after you enroll in Medicare, you can still withdraw money you've already accumulated in the account tax-free for eligible medical expenses. A few examples of this would be for health insurance deductibles and copayments, out-of-pocket costs for prescription drugs, over-the-counter medications, dental and vision care, and other costs that aren't covered by insurance. Plus, after you turn sixty-five, you can also withdraw money tax-free from the HSA for Medicare premiums, including Part B, Part D, Medicare Advantage (and Part A premiums if you have to pay them), but not Medigap premiums.

You can also withdraw HSA money tax-free for eligible long-term care insurance premiums based on your age. For more information about HSA-eligible expenses, see IRS Publication 969 at IRS.gov.

TAX-FREE HSA WITHDRAWALS
FOR FUTURE EXPENSES

HSAs are different from a flexible spending account (FSA) you may have at work. You can contribute to an HSA as long as you have an eligible high-deductible health insurance policy, whether through your employer or on your own, and you haven't enrolled in Medicare. There are no use-it-or-lose-it rules: You can keep the money growing in the account and withdraw it tax-free for eligible expenses any time in the future. Because Medicare premiums are eligible expenses, you can keep money growing in the account for years knowing that you'll have those eligible expenses after you enroll in Medicare—regardless of your other medical expenses.

If you keep your money growing in an HSA for the long term, it's a good idea to choose investments that match your time frame—such as mutual funds that invest in stocks when you have several years before you plan to use the money, while keeping money you plan to use in the short term in a money market or savings account within the HSA.

MEDICARE FOR PEOPLE WITH DISABILITIES

Qualifying for Early Medicare

Most people are eligible for Medicare starting the month they turn sixty-five. But some people qualify for Medicare before that age. About 10% of the 69 million Americans enrolled in Medicare are under age sixty-five and have a qualifying disability. Qualifying for early Medicare can be complicated, but new rules are easing the requirements for people with certain conditions.

People younger than sixty-five may qualify for Medicare after they have been entitled to Social Security Disability Insurance (SSDI) benefits for at least twenty-four months. You can also receive Medicare early if you've received disability benefits from the Railroad Retirement Board (RRB) for at least twenty-four months.

The twenty-four-month waiting period has been in place since Medicare expanded in 1972 to cover eligible people with disabilities. Since then, the government has waived the twenty-four-month waiting period for people with permanent kidney failure who require dialysis or a kidney transplant (known as end-stage renal disease) and people with amyotrophic lateral sclerosis (ALS), also known as Lou Gehrig's disease.

You will be enrolled in Medicare Part A and Part B automatically after receiving SSDI benefits for twenty-four months (unless you are eligible earlier), and you'll receive your Medicare card in the mail. You must keep Medicare Part A when enrolled automatically, but you can decide whether or not to keep Medicare Part B. Some people who have employer coverage, such as from a working spouse, choose not to keep Part B so they don't have to pay the monthly premium, even if they qualify for early coverage. You can follow the instructions on the back of the card to return it and request to enroll only in Part A.

OTHER COVERAGE TO SUPPLEMENT MEDICARE

Even though you have a disability, you may still have to pay deductibles and copayments for Medicare, and you usually won't receive prescription drug coverage automatically. You may want to sign up for prescription drug coverage through a standalone Part D plan or get your medical and drug coverage from a private Medicare Advantage plan.

You'll have an initial enrollment period to sign up for Part D or Medicare Advantage; it begins twenty-one months after you get Social Security or RRB disability benefits and lasts through the twenty-eighth month. If you sign up for Part D or Medicare Advantage before you've received disability benefits for twenty-four months, then that coverage will begin the same day your Medicare Part A and Part B coverage starts. If you sign up in the three months after your Medicare Part A and Part B coverage starts, your Part D or Medicare Advantage coverage starts the first day of the month after the plan gets your request.

In the past, people with end-stage renal disease weren't eligible to enroll in Medicare Advantage plans before age sixty-five. However, the 21st Century Cures Act, passed by Congress in 2016, changed the rules to allow people with end-stage renal disease to enroll in Medicare Advantage plans starting in 2021. That option can be particularly helpful in states that don't require insurers to offer Medigap policies to Medicare enrollees under age sixty-five. If you have Medicare Advantage, you may have to use providers in the plan's network, and you may have more prior authorization requirements. But some Medicare Advantage plans specialize in people with chronic conditions, such as kidney disease.

MEDIGAP COMPLICATIONS FOR EARLY MEDICARE

If you choose to get your coverage through Original Medicare, the government-run program where you can use any doctor who participates, you may want to get a Medigap policy to help cover your deductibles, copayments, and other out-of-pocket costs.

However, federal law doesn't require insurers to sell Medigap policies to people under age sixty-five. After age sixty-five, you can enroll in any Medigap plan available in your state within six months of enrolling in Medicare Part B, regardless of preexisting conditions. Before age sixty-five, Medigap insurers in some states may reject you for coverage or charge more because of preexisting conditions, no matter when you sign up, or they may not offer the coverage to early Medicare beneficiaries at all.

These rules vary a lot by state—some states require Medigap companies to offer at least one plan to eligible Medicare beneficiaries under the age of sixty-five, while others may only offer plans to those under sixty-five with certain conditions. See the

Medigap section at Medicare.gov for a list of states with special rules. You can contact your state's Department of Insurance (see https://content.naic.org/state-insurance-departments for contact information and links) or the State Health Insurance Assistance Program (SHIP) for more information about your state's requirements and protections. You can find your local SHIP at www.shiphelp.org.

Even if you're in a state that doesn't require Medigap insurers to sell policies to people with disabilities who qualify for Medicare early, you'll get a second chance to get Medigap when you turn sixty-five—at that point, you'll have six months to buy any Medigap policy available in your state at the best price for your age and gender.

Shopping for Medigap at Sixty-Five

Even if you qualified for Medicare early because of a disability and have a Medigap policy, take advantage of the opportunity to shop around again at sixty-five—you may find a plan with lower rates. You have six months to switch plans regardless of preexisting conditions.

Chapter 3

How to Sign Up for Medicare

After you decide when to enroll in Medicare and which parts you want to include, you need to take action to sign up. You're enrolled in Medicare automatically if you're already receiving Social Security benefits at least four months before your sixty-fifth birthday. But now that the age to receive full retirement benefits is sixty-six to sixty-seven, depending on the year you were born, most people haven't signed up for Social Security by sixty-five. That means they need to enroll themselves.

The Social Security Administration handles Medicare enrollment, and you can complete the process at www.ssa .gov/medicare/sign-up. But it can be tricky to know which forms to submit and how to add supplemental coverage. The procedure is different for people who are retired and signing up at sixty-five than it is for people who can delay enrollment while they have employer coverage.

This chapter provides a step-by-step guide for enrolling in Medicare and adding additional coverage, whether you're signing up during your initial enrollment period at sixty-five or if you qualify for a special enrollment period later—or even if you miss your enrollment deadlines. You'll also learn about resources that can help and expensive mistakes to avoid.

STEPS TO PREPARE FOR MEDICARE

Six Months Before You Turn Sixty-Five

Your Medicare coverage can start the month you turn sixty-five, but taking time to prepare beforehand can help the process go smoothly and give you a head start on your Medicare decisions. You may want to start researching and some administrative tasks six months before you turn sixty-five, so you'll be ready with your Medicare plan as soon as the coverage can take effect.

FIND OUT HOW MEDICARE WORKS WITH OTHER COVERAGE

If you have health insurance from another source—such as employer coverage, COBRA continuation coverage, retiree health insurance, military TRICARE coverage, ACA marketplace coverage, or Medicaid—find out how that coverage interacts with Medicare. In most cases, you'll need to sign up for Medicare during your initial enrollment period at sixty-five, but you may be able to keep the other coverage to help cover Medicare's out-of-pocket costs. Calculate whether it's worthwhile to keep the other coverage.

ASK YOUR EMPLOYER ABOUT OPTIONS

If you have coverage through an employer, ask your Human Resources department how your coverage works with Medicare.

Companies with twenty or more employees must let you keep your group health insurance as primary coverage even after age sixty-five. Coverage from smaller companies usually becomes secondary at sixty-five and you'll need to enroll in Medicare to avoid big gaps. But some employers have different rules; you'll need to find out from your employer how your coverage works with Medicare and what action you need to take at sixty-five.

MAKE A COVERAGE PLAN FOR A YOUNGER SPOUSE

Medicare isn't a family plan, and you may need to find new coverage for a younger spouse if you drop your current insurance when you sign up for Medicare. Your spouse may be able to stay on your former employer's plan for up to thirty-six months after you're eligible for Medicare through COBRA. The coverage remains the same as you had at work, but the premiums may jump because your spouse will have to pay both the employer's and employee's share of the cost. Another option is to get individual coverage through the ACA insurance marketplace. Your spouse may qualify for a premium subsidy to help with the cost, depending on your household income.

CREATE AN ONLINE *MY* SOCIAL SECURITY ACCOUNT

You'll need this account to sign up for Medicare online, unless you're already receiving Social Security benefits four months before you turn sixty-five—those are the only people who are enrolled automatically. You can sign up for an online Social Security account at www.ssa.gov/myaccount.

PREPARE TO ENROLL IN MEDICARE THREE MONTHS BEFORE YOU TURN SIXTY-FIVE

You can sign up for Medicare during your initial enrollment period, which starts three months before the month you turn sixty-five and lasts for three months afterward. If you sign up before your birthday month, your coverage will begin on the first of the month you turn sixty-five. (Or the previous month, if your birthday is on the first.) If you sign up during your birthday month or the three months afterward, your coverage will begin the first of the following month. Go to www.ssa.gov/medicare/sign-up to prepare for the process.

THINK ABOUT ORIGINAL MEDICARE OR MEDICARE ADVANTAGE

After you sign up for Medicare Part A and Part B, you can choose to keep coverage from Original Medicare or sign up for a private Medicare Advantage plan. This decision will determine the rest of your options and could affect your coverage for years. Start thinking about the pros and cons of each path (see the "Choose Between Original Medicare or Medicare Advantage" section in Chapter 2 for details). Find out more about the costs and coverage for the Medicare Advantage plans in your area using the Medicare.gov Plan Finder at www.medicare.gov/plan-compare.

OPTING FOR PART D OR MEDIGAP

If you choose to sign up for Original Medicare, you'll need to decide if you want to sign up for Part D and/or Medigap. You can find out more about the Part D policies available in your area using the Medicare.gov Plan Finder at www.medicare.gov/plan-compare. You can research your Medigap options using the Medigap tool at www.medicare.gov and learn about plans available in your area, as well as state consumer protections, through your state's Department of Insurance (see https://content.naic.org/state-insurance-departments for additional resources).

QUALIFYING FOR FINANCIAL ASSISTANCE

Start looking into whether you can qualify for financial assistance with Medicare Part A and Part B costs from a Medicare Savings Program or help paying your Part D premiums and deductibles through the Extra Help program. Knowing whether you are eligible for those programs may affect some of your other Medicare decisions, such as whether or not you need a Medigap policy. Visit www.medicare.gov/basics/costs/help for more information about these programs and eligibility requirements.

Get Help with Medicare Questions

You can get personalized help with Medicare questions through your local SHIP (www.shiphelp.org). There, you can learn more about the steps to sign up, how to choose a Part D or Medicare Advantage plan that covers your drug prescriptions and doctors, state Medigap consumer protections, and whether you can qualify for financial assistance. You can also get help by calling 1-800-MEDICARE.

CONTEST THE HIGH-INCOME SURCHARGE AFTER RETIRING

If your income was above a certain level when you were working, you may get a notice that your Medicare Part B and Part D premiums are higher because of the IRMAA, which is a Medicare high-income surcharge.

The Social Security Administration usually uses your last tax return on file to determine the surcharge—for example, 2024 income for 2026 premiums. But if your income has dropped since then because of certain life-changing events, including retirement, divorce, or death of a spouse, you can ask the Social Security Administration to use more recent income and reduce the surcharge. You may have to pay the surcharge while your request is being processed, but you'll get the extra money back retroactively if approved.

TAKING SOCIAL SECURITY BEFORE SIXTY-FIVE AND MEDICARE

Early Social Security Triggers Medicare Enrollment

Even though signing up for Medicare and Social Security are two separate decisions, the Social Security Administration handles Medicare enrollment, so the age when you decide to claim Social Security benefits affects the process for enrolling in Medicare.

The age for receiving full Social Security benefits had been sixty-five for a long time, but as life expectancy increased and Social Security trust funds became strained, Congress passed a law in 1983 to gradually increase the age for receiving full retirement benefits. The change was spread out over many years, rising to age sixty-five and two months for people born in 1938, and increasing by two months for each birth year—hitting age sixty-six for people born from 1943 to 1954 then gradually increasing to sixty-seven for people born in 1960 or later.

Even though you can claim Social Security benefits as early as age sixty-two rather than waiting until your full retirement age, your monthly benefits will be permanently reduced by as much as 30%. The age for Medicare eligibility remains at sixty-five, so most people haven't enrolled in Social Security by the time they need to make Medicare decisions. They need to take steps to sign up for Medicare themselves. However, enrolling is automatic for people who are receiving early Social Security benefits at sixty-five.

AUTOMATIC MEDICARE ENROLLMENT AT SIXTY-FIVE

If you're receiving Social Security retirement benefits at least four months before you turn sixty-five, you're enrolled automatically in Medicare Part A and Part B. You'll receive your Medicare card and a welcome packet in the mail three months before your sixty-fifth birthday and can start using it the first of the month you turn sixty-five (or the beginning of the previous month if your birthday is on the first). The card will specify your start date.

Railroad employees and their spouses have a separate retirement system from Social Security but similar rules for Medicare enrollment. People who are already receiving Railroad Retirement Board (RRB) benefits at sixty-five will be automatically enrolled in Railroad Medicare and will receive their card in the mail three months before their birthday. Their card looks slightly different from the standard Medicare card, but the benefits are the same.

Special Rules for Puerto Rico

If you're a resident of Puerto Rico and are already receiving Social Security benefits, you'll only be enrolled automatically in Medicare Part A but not Part B. If you want to sign up for Part B, you'll need to take steps to enroll at the Social Security Administration website or by going to a Social Security office. For more information, see the "Medicare in Puerto Rico" fact sheet available at the Social Security Administration website (www.ssa.gov/pubs/EN-05-10521.pdf).

SHOULD YOU KEEP PART B?

If you're enrolled in Medicare automatically and you want to keep both Part A and Part B, you don't need to do anything. You can just start using your Medicare card on the eligible date. Most people should keep Part A and Part B.

However, if you or your spouse are still working and you have health insurance from an employer with twenty or more employees (or other employer coverage that is primary to Medicare), you may decide to delay signing up for Part B so you don't need to pay premiums for both your employer coverage and Medicare.

You'll need to keep Part A if you're enrolled automatically. If you want to delay signing up for Part B, you can send back your Medicare card and just keep Part A. Write down your Medicare number first so you can start using Part A on the eligible date.

Follow the instructions on the back of the form the Medicare card came on and check the box that says, "I DON'T want Part B (Medical Insurance)." Sign the form and send back the card. You'll receive a new card in the mail with Part A coverage only.

You need to remember to sign up for Part B no later than eight months after losing employer coverage, or else you may have a late enrollment penalty. You can sign up online at the Social Security Administration website (www.ssa.gov/medicare/sign-up) or at your local Social Security office.

MAKE DECISIONS ABOUT COVERAGE

Even if you're enrolled automatically in Medicare, you'll still need to make decisions about other coverage and sign up for other programs separately. Each has its pros and cons that may apply differently to your individual situation.

Original Medicare or Medicare Advantage?

After you enroll in Medicare Part A and Part B, you can decide to keep coverage through Original Medicare or get a private Medicare Advantage plan, which usually has provider networks but includes medical and prescription drug coverage in one plan.

If you want to keep Original Medicare, you don't need to take any extra steps—you're automatically enrolled in that program. If you want Medicare Advantage, you'll need to choose a plan and enroll with a private company. You can compare plans in your area and sign up for Medicare Advantage by using the Plan Finder tool at Medicare.gov (www.medicare.gov/plan-compare).

Do You Need a Part D Prescription Drug Plan?

If you keep Original Medicare and don't have other prescription drug coverage, you may need to sign up for a standalone Part D prescription drug plan through a private insurer. You can also compare Part D options in your area and sign up for a plan at www.medicare .gov/plan-compare.

Do You Need Medigap?

You may want to supplement Original Medicare with a private Medigap policy that helps pay many of Medicare's out-of-pocket costs. You'll need to buy the policy from a Medigap insurer or agent. You can't be rejected or charged more because of preexisting conditions if you buy the Medigap policy within six months of enrolling in Part B at sixty-five or older.

SIGNING UP FOR MEDICARE ONLINE

Steps to Take During Your Initial Enrollment Period

Most people aren't enrolled in Medicare automatically, and they need to take steps to sign up. If you're receiving Social Security benefits at least four months before you turn sixty-five, you're enrolled in Medicare automatically. But most people haven't claimed Social Security benefits at that point because the age to receive full Social Security retirement benefits is sixty-six or older for people born in 1943 and later.

You can still enroll in Medicare at sixty-five, even if you aren't receiving Social Security benefits yet—those are two separate decisions. But you'll need to take special steps to sign up. The Medicare enrollment process is handled by the Social Security Administration, and you can sign up online at the Social Security Administration website (www.ssa.gov/medicare/sign-up) or by visiting your local Social Security Administration office (see the Office Locator at www.ssa.gov/locator).

WHEN AND HOW TO SIGN UP

Most people should sign up for Medicare during their initial enrollment period, which begins three months before the month they turn sixty-five and ends three months later. If you have other health insurance—such as through a retiree plan, small employer, COBRA continuation coverage, or TRICARE Military Health Care—that coverage usually becomes secondary to Medicare at sixty-five and you need to sign up during your initial enrollment period or you may have coverage gaps and late enrollment penalties.

Even people who have coverage from an employer with twenty or more employees often choose to enroll in Medicare Part A at sixty-five, although they may delay signing up for Part B while they're working so they don't have to pay premiums for both types of coverage.

You can enroll online during your initial enrollment period for both Part A and Part B, or for Part A only. (You'll need to follow a separate procedure to sign up for Part B during a special enrollment period no later than eight months after you lose the employer's coverage.)

The process during your initial enrollment period is simple: Go to the Medicare sign-up page (www.ssa.gov/medicare/sign-up) and click "Apply online" in the "Sign up for Medicare" section. You'll be asked to log on to your online *my* Social Security account or create one. There, you'll provide personal information, and then click "yes" where it asks whether you want to enroll in Medicare *only*—not Social Security retirement benefits. You can also specify if you want to enroll in Part B in addition to Part A. After answering a few more questions, sign the form electronically, click "submit" and you'll receive a receipt. Your Medicare card and a "Welcome to Medicare" package should arrive in the mail within two weeks. Your coverage start date is listed on the front of the card.

If you choose not to enroll online, you can visit your local Social Security Administration office to sign up.

OTHER CONSIDERATIONS

Signing up for Medicare is just the first step. You'll also need to make decisions about other plans within a certain time frame to avoid late enrollment penalties and coverage gaps.

Original Medicare or Medicare Advantage

After you enroll in Medicare Part A and Part B, you need to decide whether to keep coverage through Original Medicare or sign up for a private Medicare Advantage plan, which has provider networks but usually includes medical care and prescription drug coverage in one plan. If you want a Medicare Advantage plan, you'll need to choose a plan and enroll with a private company. You can compare plans in your area and enroll using the Plan Finder tool at Medicare.gov (www.medicare.gov/plan-compare).

Part D Prescription Drug Plan

Medicare doesn't automatically cover prescription drugs. Unless you have drug coverage from another source, called "creditable coverage," you'll need to sign up for a Medicare prescription drug plan during your initial enrollment period or within two months of losing other coverage. Otherwise, you may have to pay a late enrollment penalty. If you have Original Medicare, you can get a standalone Part D plan through a private insurer. If you choose to get coverage from a private Medicare Advantage plan, you can get Part D coverage within that plan. You can compare the options for both types of plans in your area and enroll at www.medicare.gov/plan-compare.

Medigap Policy

After you enroll in Medicare Part A and Part B, you may want to supplement Original Medicare with a Medigap policy that helps pay many of Medicare's out-of-pocket costs. You can sign up directly with the Medigap insurer or through an agent. If you buy a Medigap policy within six months of enrolling in Medicare Part

B at sixty-five or older, insurers can't reject you or charge more because of preexisting conditions.

More about Medigap

You can find out more about Medigap policies in your area by using the Medigap finder tool at Medicare.gov. Most state insurance departments have information about available policies and costs, and special consumer protections. You can find contact information for your state insurance department at the National Association of Insurance Commissioners' website (https://content .naic.org/state-insurance-departments).

SIGNING UP AFTER SIXTY-FIVE

Taking Advantage of Special Enrollment Periods

If you or your spouse were still working at sixty-five and you had health insurance from that employer, you may not have signed up for Medicare during your initial enrollment period. Or you may have signed up for premium-free Part A but delayed enrolling in Part B so you wouldn't have to pay monthly premiums for both Medicare and the employer plan.

However, you'll need to sign up for Medicare after you lose your employer coverage. You qualify for a special enrollment period that begins any time while you or your spouse are still working in the job that provides health insurance and lasts up to eight months after that job ends, and you lose the coverage. The steps to sign up during a special enrollment period are different than the proce-dure for enrolling at sixty-five.

HOW TO ENROLL IN PART B ONLINE DURING A SPECIAL ENROLLMENT PERIOD

To enroll in Medicare online during a special enrollment period, go to the Medicare sign-up page at the Social Security Administration website (www.ssa.gov/medicare/sign-up). If you already signed up for Part A but need to sign up for Part B, click on "Get started" under the section "Sign up for Part B only." Fill in and sign the Medicare

Part B online application. In the "remark" section, specify when you would like the Part B coverage to begin. It's a good idea to sign up a month before your current coverage ends so you don't have coverage gaps.

You'll also need to provide information about the employer health insurance coverage you had since you were sixty-five so you won't have to pay a late enrollment penalty. Your employer can fill out a form with the information, or you can attach documentation. See the Form CMS-L564 and Form CMS-40B for details.

You can also submit Form CMS-40B during your initial enrollment period if you live in Puerto Rico and were enrolled automatically in Part A but not Part B.

Signing Up at a Social Security Office

The Social Security Administration prefers you to sign up online. But you can also sign up by going to a local Social Security Administration office (www.ssa.gov/locator) with the forms and information from your employer.

ENROLLING IN PARTS A AND B DURING SPECIAL ENROLLMENT

You'll need to follow a different procedure if you delayed signing up for both Part A and Part B while you or your spouse were working and you had health insurance from that employer. Contact the Social Security Administration to sign up—you can either call or visit a local office (www.ssa.gov/locator). If you qualify for premium-free Part A, you can sign up at any time without penalty.

Your coverage will take effect six months retroactively, but no earlier than the month you turn sixty-five (or the first of the previous month if your birthday is on the first). You'll need to sign up for Part B no later than eight months after losing employer coverage.

ENROLL DURING A GENERAL ENROLLMENT PERIOD

If you didn't enroll in Medicare during your initial enrollment period and you don't qualify for a special enrollment period—for example, if more than eight months have passed since losing employer coverage—you'll need to wait until the general enrollment period to sign up for Part B, which runs from January 1 to March 31 each year. You may have to pay a late enrollment penalty.

You can't sign up online during a general enrollment period, but you can submit Form CMS-40B to your local Social Security office. You may also want to submit Form CMS-L564 showing that you had employer coverage during some of that time, which could reduce your late enrollment penalty.

OTHER COVERAGE DECISIONS TO MAKE

After you enroll in Medicare, you'll still need to make some additional decisions:

Original Medicare or Medicare Advantage

After you enroll in Medicare Part A and Part B, you can decide to keep coverage through Original Medicare or sign up for a private

Medicare Advantage plan. If you want Medicare Advantage, you can sign up within two months of losing employer coverage or during the annual open enrollment period.

Part D Prescription Drug Plan

If you lose prescription drug coverage when you or your spouse stop working, you'll have up to two months to sign up for a Part D plan without a late enrollment penalty.

Medigap Policy

If you choose Original Medicare, you may want to supplement that coverage with a private Medigap policy that helps pay many of Medicare's out-of-pocket costs. You may not have needed Medigap while you were working, but if you don't sign up within a certain time frame, insurers in most states can reject you or charge more because of preexisting conditions. You can qualify for a guaranteed issue period to sign up regardless of preexisting conditions if you buy Medigap within six months of enrolling in Part B, or up to two months after losing coverage that was secondary to Medicare. You can buy Medigap from the company or from an agent.

SUPPLEMENTING ORIGINAL MEDICARE

Sign Up for Medigap and Part D

If you decide to get your coverage from Original Medicare rather than a private Medicare Advantage plan, you may want to buy two additional policies: Medicare supplemental coverage (also called Medigap) and Part D prescription drug coverage. Both types of policies are offered by private insurers, and you'll have several options available in your area. If you don't sign up at certain times, you could end up with late enrollment penalties or difficulty qualifying for coverage.

WHEN TO SIGN UP FOR MEDIGAP

You can buy a Medigap policy after you sign up for both Medicare Part A and Part B. Unlike Medicare Advantage and Part D, there is no annual open enrollment period for Medigap; you are given a one-time Medigap open enrollment period, when you can buy any Medigap policy available in your area, which lasts for six months upon first receiving your Part B coverage. If you buy a policy after that six-month period, insurers in most states can reject you for coverage or charge more because of preexisting conditions, making this different than all other Medicare-related coverages. However, as long as you continue to pay premiums, you can keep the policy even if you develop a medical condition.

Guaranteed Issue Rights

If you don't sign up for Medigap within six months of enrolling in Medicare Part B at age sixty-five or older, Medigap insurers in most states can reject you or charge more because of preexisting conditions. However, there are certain situations, called guaranteed issue rights, when insurers must offer you certain Medigap policies, regardless of your health.

For example, if you have other insurance that is secondary to Medicare—such as from a small employer, retiree coverage, or COBRA continuation coverage—you can qualify for guaranteed issue rights for sixty-three days after losing secondary coverage, and Medigap insurers must offer you most policies regardless of preexisting conditions.

You also qualify for guaranteed issue rights in several other situations. For example, if you change your mind within the first year of joining a Medicare Advantage plan, you can switch to Original Medicare and get a Medigap policy. Or, if you move out of a Medicare Advantage plan's service area, you can switch to Original Medicare and have sixty-three days to get most Medigap policies.

See the Medigap open enrollment page at www.medicare .gov/health-drug-plans/medigap/ready-to-buy for other guaranteed issue rights.

States with Special Rules

Medigap is regulated by the states, and a few states have different rules about preexisting conditions. Three states—Connecticut, Massachusetts, and New York—let you buy a Medigap policy at any time regardless of preexisting conditions. Maine requires Medigap insurers to offer Medigap Plan A to all residents age sixty-five and older for one month every year (the insurer decides which month that will be). Several states require Medigap insurers to let you buy a policy or switch plans without any health questions each year during your birthday month. For example, California lets you switch from one Medigap policy to another one with the same or lesser benefits within sixty days after your birthday each year; Maryland gives you thirty days.

You can find out more about your state's rules from your local SHIP office (www.shiphelp.org) or your state's Department of Insurance (https://content.naic.org/state-insurance-departments).

Buying a Medigap Policy

If you don't buy a Medigap policy within six months after enrolling in Medicare Part B and you don't qualify for other guaranteed issue rights, you'll usually need to fill out a medical questionnaire before you can buy a Medigap policy. The impact of different medical conditions on your acceptance and premiums can vary a lot by company.

Generally, the older you are when you buy the policy, the higher the premiums. Some companies and states have community-rated policies, where everyone in the area pays the same premiums regardless of age.

Using a Medigap Agent

In addition to buying Medigap online or directly from the insurance company, you can also buy Medigap from a licensed insurance agent, which may be helpful if you don't qualify for guaranteed issue rights. The agent can help you present your case and find an insurer that tends to offer the best rates for someone with your medical conditions. Your state insurance department can help you find licensed agents in your area (https://content.naic.org/state-insurance-departments).

You can buy a Medigap policy directly from the insurer—the Medigap finder at Medicare.gov lists companies and cost estimates (search for "Find a Medigap policy that works for you"). You can also find a list of Medigap insurers at most state insurance department websites.

WHEN TO SIGN UP FOR PART D PRESCRIPTION DRUG COVERAGE

The rules for signing up for Part D are very different than they are for Medigap. You can only buy a Part D plan at certain times, but you can get any plan available in your area, and you'll pay the same rate regardless of your health, age, or gender.

You can sign up for Part D during your initial enrollment period after signing up for Medicare Part A or Part B. You can also sign up or switch plans each year during open enrollment from October 15 to December 7 for coverage starting January 1. Remember to stay on top of deadlines: If you go sixty-three days or more after your initial enrollment period without creditable drug coverage from another source, you may have to pay a late enrollment penalty.

Special Enrollment Periods for Part D

You can also sign up or switch Part D plans at other times. For example:

- If you move out of the plan's coverage area or lose other coverage, you have two months to get a new Part D plan.

- You can enroll in a Part D plan with a five-star quality rating any time during the year (to find out if any five-star plans are available in your area, visit www.medicare.gov/plan-compare).
- If you qualify for the Extra Help program, which helps low-income people with Part D costs, you may be able to switch Part D policies as often as once per month.

See "Special Enrollment Periods" at Medicare.gov (www medicare.gov/basics/get-started-with-medicare/get-more-coverage/joining-a-plan/special-enrollment-periods) for a full list of these enrollment windows for Part D.

Buying Part D

You can buy a Part D plan through the Medicare.gov Plan Finder (www.medicare.gov/plan-compare). Enter your zip code and type your drugs and dosages into the Plan Finder to estimate how much you'd pay in premiums plus out-of-pocket costs for your medications for each plan available in your area. After you choose the best plan for you, you can buy the coverage through the Plan Finder. Click "Enroll" by the plan's name and provide your Medicare number, effective dates, and other information. You can also contact the insurance company or buy the coverage from a licensed insurance agent, but it's a good idea to compare the costs and coverage for all the plans in your area using the Plan Finder first, so you know about your options.

WHEN TO SIGN UP FOR MEDICARE ADVANTAGE

Steps for Enrolling in a Private Plan

After you sign up for Medicare Part A and Part B, you need to decide whether you want coverage from Original Medicare, the government-run program where you can use any doctor who participates, or a private Medicare Advantage plan, which has provider networks. Medicare Advantage plans provide all-in-one coverage—most plans cover medical expenses and prescription drugs as well as some coverage for dental, hearing, and vision care. If you sign up for a Medicare Advantage plan, you usually don't have to buy additional policies.

WHEN CAN YOU SIGN UP FOR MEDICARE ADVANTAGE?

You can sign up for a Medicare Advantage plan during your initial enrollment period for Medicare, which starts three months before the month you turn sixty-five and lasts for three months afterward. You must sign up for Medicare Part A and Part B before you can buy a Medicare Advantage plan.

You don't have to buy a Medicare Advantage plan when you first enroll in Medicare—if not, you will still have coverage from Original Medicare. After your initial enrollment period is over, you can only sign up for Medicare Advantage at limited times.

You can get a Medicare Advantage plan or switch plans during the open enrollment period, which runs from October 15 to December 7 for new coverage starting January 1. Even if you already have a Medicare Advantage plan, it's a good idea to compare your options each year during open enrollment—plans can change their provider networks, covered drugs, premiums, and other costs and coverage each year. The plan you chose the previous year may no longer be your best option. (See Choosing a Medicare Advantage Plan in Chapter 4 for guidance on selecting a plan.) After you have a Medicare Advantage plan, you can also switch plans from January 1 to March 31 each year or leave Medicare Advantage for Original Medicare.

MEDICARE ADVANTAGE SPECIAL ENROLLMENT PERIODS

You can also sign up or switch Medicare Advantage plans during other special times, for example:

- You can switch plans or leave Medicare Advantage for Original Medicare within two months of moving out of the plan's service area. This is helpful because your providers may no longer be covered in the plan's network if you move to a different area.
- You can get a Medicare Advantage plan within two months after losing other coverage, such as an employer plan.
- You can get a Medicare Advantage plan with a five-star quality rating any time during the year. The five-star special enrollment period runs from December 8 to November 30 of the following year, and the one week not included is during the annual open enrollment period. Type your zip code into the Medicare Plan

Finder (www.medicare.gov/plan-compare) to see if there are any five-star plans available in your area.

These are just a few examples of when you can opt for Medicare Advantage; see "Special Enrollment Periods" at Medicare.gov (www.medicare.gov/basics/get-started-with-medicare/get-more-coverage/joining-a-plan/special-enrollment-periods) for a full list of other windows.

REMEMBER MEDIGAP WHEN LEAVING MEDICARE ADVANTAGE

Even though you can leave a Medicare Advantage plan and return to Original Medicare pretty easily (you can disenroll from your plan and return to Original Medicare during the annual open enrollment period from October 15 to December 7, or the Medicare Advantage open enrollment period from January 1 to March 31 and during special enrollment periods), you may have a difficult time getting a Medigap policy to supplement Original Medicare. Unless you buy a Medigap policy within six months of signing up for Medicare Part B or during other times when you have guaranteed issue rights, insurers in most states can reject you for coverage or charge more because of preexisting conditions. You are not guaranteed to qualify for Medigap coverage if you leave a Medicare Advantage plan during one of these open enrollment periods.

Think carefully before signing up for a Medicare Advantage plan because it could be a long-term decision—consider your current and potential healthcare costs in the future. Also keep in mind the guaranteed issue periods for Medigap. For example, when you first sign up for Medicare Advantage, you have a twelve-month trial period; if you're dissatisfied, you can return to Original Medicare and qualify for any Medigap plan (and insurers cannot deny you for Medigap coverage or charge you a higher rate). If you decide to drop a Medigap policy and switch to Medicare Advantage, you'll have up to twelve months to return to Original Medicare and reclaim that Medigap policy (but only if the insurance company still sells that same policy). See the Medigap section at Medicare.gov (www.medicare.gov/health-drug-plans/medigap/ready-to-buy) for other guaranteed issue rights.

In a few states—including Connecticut, Massachusetts, and New York—you can get a Medigap policy at other times regardless of your health. In that case, there's less risk of choosing a Medicare Advantage plan and changing your mind later.

SIGNING UP FOR MEDICARE ADVANTAGE

Most people have many Medicare Advantage plans to choose from in their area—the average Medicare beneficiary has thirty-two Medicare Advantage plans with health and drug coverage to choose from in 2026, according to KFF, a healthcare policy and research organization. You can learn about all the plans available in your area with the Medicare Plan Finder tool (www.medicare.gov/plan-compare). After you choose a plan, you can enroll from the Plan Finder, or you can contact the company directly or buy coverage through a licensed agent. If you need assistance enrolling or choosing a plan, take advantage of SHIP, the State Health Insurance Assistance Program (www.shiphelp.org).

MEDICARE COST-REDUCING PROGRAMS

Financial Help with Premiums and More

Even though Medicare can cover many of your healthcare costs after you turn sixty-five, you'll still have to pay premiums, deductibles, and copayments for Part A and Part B. Plus, you may have additional premiums if you have a Medicare Advantage plan or a standalone Part D and Medigap plan to provide supplemental coverage. Luckily, several programs can help with some of these expenses. However, eligibility is based on income and, sometimes, on assets.

MEDICARE SAVINGS PROGRAMS

These programs outlined in this entry help cover Medicare Part A and Part B premiums, deductibles, and copayments. On a base level, there are four types of Medicare Savings Programs, and eligibility can vary by state. Some states don't count savings or other assets when determining eligibility, while other states do consider your assets. You should contact your state Medicaid office for details on these programs (www.medicaid.gov/about-us/where-can-people-get-help-medicaid-chip#statemenu). Puerto Rico and the US Virgin Islands don't have these Medicare Savings Programs.

Qualified Medicare Beneficiary Program

This program helps pay for Part A and Part B premiums, deductibles, coinsurance, and copayments. Additionally, you automatically qualify for the Extra Help program that helps with Part D prescription drug expenses. For example, in 2025 you pay $12.15 or less for each drug covered by your plan.

In 2025, the federal income and asset limits to qualify for this plan are:

- Individuals: $1,325 monthly income; $9,660 assets
- Married couples: $1,783 monthly income; $14,470 assets

See the "Medicare Savings Programs" page at www.medicare .gov/basics/costs/help/medicare-savings-programs for updated federal income and asset amounts. Some states have higher limits.

Specified Low-Income Medicare Beneficiary Program

The Specified Low-Income Medicare Beneficiary Program has slightly higher income limits and pays Part B premiums but not the deductibles and copayments. This program also makes you eligible for the Part D Extra Help program, where you pay no more than $12.15 in 2025 for each drug covered by your plan.

In 2025, the federal income and asset limits to qualify for this plan are:

- Individuals: $1,585 monthly income; $9,660 assets
- Married couples: $2,135 monthly income; $14,470 assets

Some states have higher limits.

Qualifying Individual Program

This program has the highest income levels to qualify. It pays the Part B premiums and enables you to participate in the Part D Extra Help program. States approve these applications on a first-come, first-served basis.

In 2025, the federal income and asset limits to qualify for this plan are:

- Individuals: $1,781 monthly income; $9,660 assets
- Married couples: $2,400 monthly income; $14,470 assets

Some states have higher limits.

Qualified Disabled and Working Individual Program

This program is for a very limited group: People with disabilities who return to work and lose Social Security disability benefits, and then don't qualify for premium-free Medicare Part A because they don't have enough Social Security work credits. The program helps to pay their Part A premiums while they earn the credits toward premium-free Part A.

In 2025, the federal income and asset limits to qualify for this plan are:

- Individuals: $5,302 monthly income; $4,000 assets
- Married couples: $7,135 monthly income; $6,000 assets

Some states have higher limits.

Signing Up for a Medicare Savings Program

Contact your state Medicaid program or your local SHIP office for the steps to apply for a Medicare Savings Program in your state. When you sign up for the Extra Help program to assist with prescription drug costs, your application is automatically forwarded to the state to determine whether you are eligible for a Medicare Savings Program too.

For more information about Medicare Savings Programs and current income limits, see "Medicare Savings Programs" at Medicare.gov (www.medicare.gov/basics/costs/help/medicare-savings-programs).

EXTRA HELP FOR
PRESCRIPTION DRUGS

The Extra Help program, also called the Low-Income Subsidy program, helps pay premiums, deductibles, and copayments for Part D prescription drug coverage. You apply for the Extra Help program through the Social Security Administration website (www.ssa.gov/medicare/part-d-extra-help). If you are enrolled in a Medicare Savings Program, you automatically qualify for this additional program.

You generally need to have income and assets below a certain limit to qualify for the Extra Help program, and those limits can change each year. In 2025, the income limit is $23,475 and the resource limit (the value of your assets, such as bank accounts and mutual funds) is $17,600 for individuals. For married couples, the income limit is $31,725, and the resource limit is $35,130. See "Extra Help" at Medicare.gov (www.medicare.gov/basics/costs/

help/drug-costs) for current limits. The limits are higher in Alaska and Hawaii.

If you qualify for Extra Help in 2025, you'll pay $0 in premiums and a $0 deductible for Medicare Part D. You'll pay up to $4.90 for each generic drug and up to $12.15 for each brand-name drug you fill at one of your Part D plan's participating pharmacies.

When your total drug costs reach $2,100 in 2026, including payments made on your behalf through the Extra Help program, you'll pay $0 for each covered drug.

If you don't already have a Part D plan, you'll be enrolled in one automatically if you receive full Medicaid coverage, are enrolled in a Medicare Savings Program, or receive Supplemental Security Income (SSI) payments from Social Security. If you are eligible for Extra Help, you can change Part D plans as often as once per month in some cases. You can also change Part D plans during open enrollment from October 15 to December 7 for new coverage starting January 1 of the following year.

You can apply for the Extra Help program through the Social Security Administration website (www.ssa.gov/medicare/part-d-extra-help). Click "Apply online" and answer several questions about eligibility, provide your Social Security number and other personal information, and details about your income and assets. You'll need to have your bank statements and tax returns, retirement account balances, and information about other income available when you fill out the forms. You can also call 1-800-772-1213 to set up an appointment with the Social Security Administration to apply for Extra Help.

To find out more about eligibility—including detailed lists of what qualifies as income and assets—and the steps for signing up, see the Understanding the *Extra Help* with Your Medicare

Prescription Drug Plan booklet at the Social Security Administration website (www.ssa.gov/pubs/EN-05-10508.pdf).

You can find out more about these and other programs to help with Medicare and drug costs in your area from your local SHIP office.

Shopping for Part D Plans

You can use the Medicare Plan Finder at www.medicare.gov/plan-compare to find out how each Part D plan in your area covers your medications. Even though Extra Help can help pay for your Part D premiums and out-of-pocket costs, it's still important to make sure that the drugs you take are on the formulary for the plan you select.

LOCATING RESOURCES FOR MEDICARE DECISIONS

Helping You Understand Enrollment and Plan Questions

Enrolling in Medicare and choosing the best combination of plans can be complicated; many of the decisions you have to make are personal and the best answer can vary depending on your circumstances. Fortunately, there are several great resources that can explain your Medicare options and help with your decisions—including some free personalized assistance to answer your questions.

THE CENTERS FOR MEDICARE & MEDICAID SERVICES AND MEDICARE.GOV

The Centers for Medicare & Medicaid Services (CMS) is the government agency that runs the Medicare program. Its Medicare.gov site is filled with information and resources to help you learn about Medicare. The site includes interactive tools to help with enrollment decisions and clearly explains the rules and costs. The Plan Finder (www.medicare.gov/plan-compare) is the best way to learn about the costs and coverage for the Part D and Medicare Advantage plans available in your area each year. You can input your zip code and prescriptions to find out how much you'd pay in premiums and out-of-pocket costs for your specific medications under each plan. You can also sign up for Part D and Medicare Advantage plans at Medicare.gov. Additionally, Medicare.gov's "What's covered?" tool (www.medicare.gov/coverage) makes it easy to look up detailed coverage rules for dozens of medical services.

You can print your Medicare card and get details about your coverage and plans by signing up for an online Medicare account. You can also call 1-800-MEDICARE (1-800-633-4227) or use the Live Chat function for help with Medicare questions.

Great Resource: "Medicare & You" Handbook

The "Medicare & You" handbook, which is updated every year, includes information about the program's current costs, coverage, and changes. Medicare beneficiaries receive the handbook each year, and you can get a copy in your online Medicare account or download a copy from the Medicare website (www.medicare.gov/medicare-and-you).

STATE HEALTH INSURANCE ASSISTANCE PROGRAMS (SHIP)

These programs provide free Medicare assistance in every state. You can call or email your local SHIP office to receive personalized help with your questions about Medicare enrollment, choosing a Part D or Medicare Advantage plan, using your coverage, and special rules and resources available in your state. Most SHIP offices also hold in-person and virtual seminars during open enrollment with information about new rules, changes to Part D and Medicare

Advantage plans in your area, and guidance on choosing a plan. Find your local SHIP office at www.shiphelp.org or call 1-877-839-2675.

THE SOCIAL SECURITY ADMINISTRATION'S WEBSITE

The Social Security Administration handles Medicare enrollment and some other administrative issues, such as applying for the Extra Help program for Part D financial assistance and appealing the Income-Related Monthly Adjustment Amount (IRMAA), the Medicare high-income surcharge. The website's Medicare section (www.ssa.gov/medicare) is filled with information about what Medicare covers and when to sign up for Part A and Part B, including a tool that shows you when your initial enrollment period starts and ends. You can sign up for Medicare online at the Social Security Administration website or visit a local Social Security office (www.ssa.gov/locator).

MEDICARE RIGHTS CENTER

The Medicare Rights Center, a nonprofit consumer service organization, has been helping people with Medicare questions and decisions for more than thirty-five years. Its Medicare Interactive website (www.medicareinteractive.org) provides online resources explaining how Medicare works, how to sign up, and how to make Medicare decisions. The main website (www.medicarerights.org) includes news about Medicare policy changes and other resources. You can call the organization's national helpline at 1-800-333-4114 to contact a counselor who can answer questions about Medicare enrollment, plan choices, coverage, and claims.

STATE INSURANCE DEPARTMENTS

Medicare is regulated by the federal government, but some states have special resources and consumer protections. The states also regulate Medigap plans, and their websites often include information about the plans and prices available in the area and state-specific rules. The National Association of Insurance Commissioners (NAIC) website includes links and contact information for each state insurance department (https://content.naic.org/state-insurance-departments).

KFF WEBSITE

This nonprofit healthcare research and policy organization (previously known as the Kaiser Family Foundation) doesn't provide one-on-one counseling, but its website (www.kff.org) is filled with information about how Medicare works, regulation changes, new coverage developments, and a detailed analysis about the Part D and Medicare Advantage plans available every year.

CENTER FOR MEDICARE ADVOCACY

The website for this nonprofit advocacy organization (https://medicareadvocacy.org) includes detailed information about

Medicare eligibility and enrollment, coverage, claims, and updates on new regulations. You can also find self-help packets for appealing Medicare claims denials and dealing with prior authorization requests.

CALIFORNIA HEALTH ADVOCATES

This nonprofit advocacy organization is focused on California, but its website (https://cahealthadvocates.org) includes information and news alerts that can help Medicare beneficiaries throughout the country. The organization also provides education for the state's Health Insurance Counseling & Advocacy Program (HICAP) counselors, which is California's SHIP program.

THE COMMONWEALTH FUND

This healthcare research foundation (www.commonwealthfund .org/medicare) includes timely studies and analysis about Medicare coverage, rule changes, and policy issues. Its Medicare data hub is filled with statistics about Medicare, costs, plans, and solvency.

COMMON ENROLLMENT MISTAKES

Avoid Errors, Gaps, and Late Penalties

Medicare can be complicated, and it's easy to make mistakes. There's a lot at stake—not only could you end up with expensive coverage gaps if you don't sign up at the right time, but you may also have to pay late enrollment penalties that last for your lifetime. This entry introduces some of the most common mistakes people make when enrolling in Medicare and steps to take to avoid these costly errors.

NOT REALIZING YOU HAVE TO SIGN UP

Even though you're eligible for Medicare at sixty-five, most people aren't enrolled automatically. Only people who are receiving early Social Security benefits at least four months before their sixty-fifth birthday will be auto-enrolled. Everyone else needs to take steps to sign up. Now that the age for receiving full Social Security benefits is over sixty-six, most people need to proactively enroll in Medicare themselves. The Social Security Administration handles Medicare enrollment, and you can sign up at www.ssa.gov/medicare or by visiting your local Social Security office. As a reminder: You don't need to claim Social Security benefits in order to sign up for Medicare.

MISSING ENROLLMENT DEADLINES

Unless you or your spouse are working at sixty-five and you have health insurance from a current employer, you generally need to sign up for Medicare during your initial enrollment period, which starts three months before the month you turn sixty-five and lasts for three months afterward. If you miss that deadline, you may have to pay a late enrollment penalty for Part B that lasts as long as you have Medicare coverage—usually for your lifetime.

DELAYING MEDICARE IF YOU HAVE SECONDARY COVERAGE

You won't have to pay a late penalty if you have coverage from your or your spouse's current employer at sixty-five, but other types of coverage don't count. If you have retiree coverage or you continued your employer's coverage through COBRA after you stopped working, you'll still need to sign up for Medicare during your initial enrollment period to avoid late enrollment penalties and coverage gaps. Coverage that isn't from a current employer becomes secondary to Medicare at sixty-five. If you don't sign up for Medicare then, you may have coverage gaps or the other insurance may not pay out at all.

NOT PAYING ATTENTION TO YOUR EMPLOYER'S SIZE

Even if you or your spouse are still working and have health insurance from a current employer, you may still need to sign up for Medicare at sixty-five; it depends on the size of your employer. Coverage from companies that have twenty or more employees can continue to be primary coverage, and you won't have coverage gaps if you don't sign up for Medicare at sixty-five (although many people working for large employers still enroll in Part A when it's premium-free). But if a company has fewer than twenty employees, that coverage typically becomes secondary to Medicare when you turn sixty-five. You won't receive a late enrollment penalty since you have coverage from a current employer, but you may have coverage gaps—or the employer's insurance may not pay at all—if you don't sign up for Medicare at sixty-five. Ask your employer about its rules.

FORGETTING TO SIGN UP AFTER LEAVING YOUR JOB

If you delay signing up for Medicare because you or your spouse are still working at sixty-five, don't forget to sign up for Medicare within eight months of leaving that job and losing the employer coverage. If you don't sign up during that special enrollment period, you'll have to wait until the next general enrollment period to sign up (January 1 to March 31 each year) and you may have to pay a late enrollment penalty.

NOT SIGNING UP FOR MEDIGAP WHEN YOU ENROLL IN PART B

You can't wait very long if you want to get a Medigap policy to help cover Original Medicare's deductibles, copayments, and other out-of-pocket costs. If you buy a policy within six months of signing up for Part B, you can get any Medigap policy in your state at the best rate for your age and gender. But after that time, insurers in most states can reject you for coverage or charge more if you have pre-existing conditions. Understand the rules in your state and other situations that could make you eligible for a Medigap policy regardless of your health.

BELIEVING IT'S EASY TO REJOIN ORIGINAL MEDICARE

Even though you can switch from a private Medicare Advantage plan back to Original Medicare during the annual open enrollment period from October 15 to December 7, you may have a difficult time getting a Medigap policy if more than six months have passed since you signed up for Part B. You may be able to get a Medigap policy regardless of your health if you change your mind and switch to Original Medicare within twelve months of first signing up for Medicare Advantage. But after that trial period is over, you may not be able to get a Medigap policy. Understand the rules in your state before choosing a Medicare Advantage plan.

NOT CHECKING THE PART D FORMULARY EVERY YEAR

Medicare Part D prescription drug coverage improved significantly in 2025, when a $2,000 annual out-of-pocket spending cap took effect (the limit rose to $2,100 in 2026). But only drugs that are covered by your plan are included in that cap. Drugs that aren't on the plan's formulary aren't covered by the plan and those expenses aren't subject to the cap. Check the plan's formulary before choosing a Part D plan during the annual open enrollment period.

Part D Formulary

A Medicare prescription drug plan formulary is its list of covered drugs. Formularies can change each year, so you can't assume that your drugs will continue to be covered on the plan's formulary each year.

Chapter 4

Choosing Your Best Coverage and Filling In the Gaps

Signing up for Medicare is the first step, but then you need to make important decisions about how to fill in the coverage gaps. You can get extra policies to cover Medicare's deductibles, copayments, and prescription drug costs, and you may have many choices for Part D prescription drug coverage, Medigap policies, or private Medicare Advantage plans in your area.

Choosing the best plans for your situation can be very personal based on your healthcare needs, medications you take, doctors you want to see, and the costs in your area. The best policy for you may be different than it is for your friends or neighbors. Some of the decisions you make when you first enroll in Medicare may affect your options for years to come.

In this chapter, you'll learn more about the steps to take and resources to help choose the best policies for you at the best price, what you need to review each year, how to switch plans if your healthcare or prescription drug needs change, and when you can change plans midyear.

WHAT MEDICARE DOESN'T COVER

How to Fill In the Gaps

You may be surprised by some of the expenses Medicare doesn't cover, especially when you consider some of the primary needs of older adults: It doesn't automatically cover prescription drugs, and it only covers dental, vision, and hearing care in limited circumstances. Medicare also leaves out one of the most significant expenses—long-term care—which can decimate your retirement savings. This entry addresses several key components that aren't covered by Medicare and how to protect your finances from these expenses.

DEDUCTIBLES, COPAYMENTS, AND OTHER OUT-OF-POCKET COSTS

If you have Original Medicare but no supplemental coverage, you may have to pay thousands of dollars for Medicare's deductibles, copayments, and coinsurance.

Medicare Part B pays 80% of the Medicare-approved cost of doctors' services and outpatient care, leaving you to pay 20% of the cost after the annual deductible ($257 in 2025). Medicare Part A has a deductible before it covers the first sixty days in the hospital ($1,676 in 2025) and you have to pay part of the cost for days sixty-one to ninety ($419 per day in 2025) and even more for longer hospital stays.

If you have retiree health insurance or TRICARE for Life for military retirees, those policies can help cover your out-of-pocket costs. Otherwise, you may want to get a Medigap policy, which can cover most of Medicare's deductibles and copayments.

Another option is to get a private Medicare Advantage plan, which must provide at least as much coverage as Original Medicare but can have different out-of-pocket costs. Details vary by plan—for example, you may pay $460 for each of the first five days in the hospital rather than the Part A deductible.

Unlike Original Medicare, Medicare Advantage plans have an out-of-pocket spending limit for medical care. In 2026, the maximum limit is $9,250 for in-network services and $13,900 for plans that cover in-network and out-of-network services. Some plans have lower limits.

The Difference Between Copayment and Coinsurance

Copayments and coinsurance are ways to calculate your portion of the costs for medical care after insurance pays its share. A copayment is typically a fixed dollar amount, such as $50 for X-rays. Coinsurance is a percentage of the cost, such as 20% of the cost of a doctor's visit.

PRESCRIPTION DRUGS

Medicare doesn't automatically cover prescription drugs, other than a few drugs that are administered in a doctor's office, such as some types of chemotherapy. You may have drug coverage if you have retiree health insurance, TRICARE for Life, or an employer plan. If not, you can buy a standalone Medicare Part D plan to supplement Original Medicare, or a Medicare Advantage plan with prescription drug coverage. Both plans have a $2,100 annual out-of-pocket spending gap for covered drugs in 2026.

DENTAL CARE

Original Medicare doesn't cover dental care except in rare circumstances, such as a dental exam before organ transplant surgery, cardiac valve replacement, or as part of Medicare-covered treatments for head and neck cancer. You need to find other coverage or pay out-of-pocket for dental exams, dental work, dentures, implants, and other dental care.

Most Medicare Advantage plans provide some dental coverage, but the details vary a lot by plan. They may cover preventive dental services without copayments, and you may have to pay 30% to 50% of the cost of more extensive dental services, such as fillings, extractions, and root canals. They may also have an annual coverage cap, such as $1,500 or higher with some plans, and you have to pay the full cost of non-preventive dental care after reaching that limit. You can also think about buying a standalone dental insurance policy or participating in a dental discount program.

HEARING CARE AND HEARING AIDS

Original Medicare doesn't cover hearing care except in limited situations, and the program does not cover hearing aids or exams for fitting them. However, Medicare does cover diagnostic hearing and balance exams ordered by your doctor to find out if you need medical treatment. It also covers cochlear implants in certain situations.

Medicare Advantage plans generally provide some hearing coverage, including an annual hearing test. They may also help pay for hearing aids—often with a copayment of a few hundred dollars or a maximum coverage cap.

Some state Medicaid programs provide hearing coverage if you meet income and other eligibility requirements. The US Department of Veterans Affairs covers hearing aids and some hearing services for eligible veterans.

Some people with moderate hearing loss can save money by buying over-the-counter hearing aids, which the US Food and Drug Administration (FDA) approved in 2022.

VISION CARE AND EYEGLASSES

Original Medicare doesn't cover eyeglasses or vision care except in certain circumstances—such as cataract surgery and glaucoma screening for high-risk patients. However, most Medicare Advantage plans cover eye exams and eyeglasses, usually with an annual coverage limit. You could also choose to get a standalone vision plan or buy a pair of discount eyeglasses.

WEIGHT LOSS DRUGS

Medicare prescription drug plans are prohibited from covering drugs prescribed specifically for weight loss. They may cover drugs like Ozempic for other FDA-approved purposes, such as for diabetes. Your doctor usually needs to complete prior authorization forms to show that you need the medications for those other FDA-approved reasons.

FOREIGN TRAVEL EMERGENCY CARE

Original Medicare doesn't cover medical care outside of the United States, except in rare circumstances—such as if you have an emergency in the United States but a foreign hospital is closest. Otherwise, you could end up with thousands of dollars of expenses if you get sick or injured while traveling—especially if you need emergency evacuation.

Most Medigap plans cover 80% of the cost of foreign travel emergency care up to a $50,000 lifetime limit, after a $250 deductible. Some Medicare Advantage plans provide limited foreign travel emergency coverage. Additionally, TRICARE for Life covers some healthcare outside the United States. Finally, travel insurance can help cover medical expenses and emergency evacuation; check on preexisting condition exclusions and coverage limits.

LONG-TERM CARE

One of the most expensive coverage gaps is long-term care. Medicare won't cover the cost of a nursing home or assisted living facility if you only need custodial care—help with the activities of daily living, such as bathing, dressing, and eating.

You can buy a long-term care insurance policy or a hybrid policy that covers both long-term care and life insurance. If you have low assets and income, Medicaid can pay some long-term care expenses. Eligible veterans can get help with long-term care expenses from the VA.

CHOOSING A PART D PRESCRIPTION DRUG PLAN

How to Find the Best Policy for You

Medicare doesn't automatically cover prescription drugs, but you can buy a Part D plan from a private insurer to help with these costs. If you have Original Medicare, the government-run program, you can get a standalone Part D plan. If you have all-in-one coverage from a Medicare Advantage plan, drug coverage is usually included in the plan.

You have several Part D plan choices. In 2026, Medicare beneficiaries have eight to twelve standalone Part D options depending on their state, according to KFF. Coverage and costs for your medications can vary a lot; the plan that works well for your friend or neighbor may not be the best one for you.

You can get a Part D plan when you first enroll in Medicare or lose other drug coverage, and you can switch plans during the annual open enrollment period from October 15 to December 7 for coverage starting January 1. Coverage and costs can change from year to year, and the drugs you take can also change. It's important to compare your options each year.

SIX FACTORS TO CONSIDER WHEN CHOOSING YOUR PLAN

The government sets a general framework for Part D coverage, and the Inflation Reduction Act of 2022 changed the structure of Part

D plans significantly starting in 2025. Part D plans must now cap annual out-of-pocket costs for covered drugs ($2,100 in 2026, adjusted annually for inflation). But your total expenses can still vary depending on the plan you choose. Here's what to look for when choosing a standalone Part D plan under the new rules:

Premiums

Average premiums for standalone Part D plans are $34.50 per month in 2026, according to the Centers for Medicare & Medicaid Services. But premiums can vary significantly depending on the plan. Some plans charge less than $5 per month while others charge more than $100. Premiums are not included in the $2,100 cap.

Deductible

You must pay the deductible before most Part D coverage kicks in. The maximum Part D deductible changes each year; it's $615 in 2026, although some plans have lower deductibles. The amount you pay for covered drugs in the deductible counts toward the $2,100 cap.

Formulary

A formulary is the plan's list of covered medications, and it's the most important factor when choosing a Part D plan. If your medication isn't included in the plan's formulary, you'll have to pay the full cost yourself, and those expenses won't be subject to the $2,100 cap.

Plans can change their formularies from year to year, so you can't assume your drugs will continue to be covered. Check the plan's formulary each year during open enrollment.

Cost Sharing for Your Medications

Most Part D plans have four or five pricing tiers, which charge different copayments (a fixed cost for the drug) or coinsurance (a percentage of the cost) for each medication on their formularies.

For example, you may pay $0 for preferred generic drugs or $5 for a thirty-day supply of other generics, or you may pay 20% of the cost of preferred brand-name drugs or 40% for non-preferred drugs. Your drugs may be preferred in one plan and non-preferred in another, which could make a big difference in your out-of-pocket costs until you reach the $2,100 cap.

New Cost-Smoothing Program

If you have a lot of drug expenses, you could reach the $2,100 out-of-pocket spending cap in the first few months of the year. A new cost-smoothing program that took effect in 2025, called the Medicare Prescription Payment Plan, can help you spread your out-of-pocket costs throughout the year. You can sign up for this free program through your drug plan at any time, and your expenses will be divided into monthly charges for the rest of the year.

Coverage Restrictions

A plan may not automatically cover all drugs on its formulary. More plans are adding restrictions to coverage. Prior authorization and step therapy are two of the most common types of coverage restrictions.

With prior authorization, your doctor must explain why you need the medication. For example, many Part D plans cover Ozempic for diabetes, but they don't cover the drug when prescribed solely for weight loss. You may find Ozempic on a plan's formulary, but your doctor may need to submit paperwork showing that you meet the criteria before it will be covered.

With step therapy, the insurer may require you to try a less expensive medication to treat a condition before approving a more expensive drug, even if both drugs are on the plan's formulary.

Preferred Pharmacies

Your costs can vary based on the pharmacy you use. Some Part D plans charge lower cost-sharing amounts for preferred pharmacies than for other in-network pharmacies. Your drugs may not be covered if you use an out-of-network pharmacy.

STRATEGIES FOR CHOOSING A PART D PLAN

You can compare these factors for the plans in your area at Medicare.gov (click on "Find health & drug plans" or go to www .medicare.gov/plan-compare). Enter your drugs and dosages into the tool to see the total premiums plus out-of-pocket costs you'd pay for the year with each plan. People who already have Medicare can receive information on their current medications by logging on to their online Medicare account.

Get Help from SHIP

If you'd like personalized help choosing a plan, contact your local State Health Insurance Assistance Program (SHIP) office. SHIP offers free Medicare assistance over the phone and sometimes in person, especially during open enrollment. Go to www.shiphelp.org to find your local SHIP.

CHOOSING A MEDICARE ADVANTAGE PLAN

Combing Through Coverage, Costs, Providers, and Drugs

If you choose to get coverage from a private Medicare Advantage plan rather than Original Medicare, you typically have several choices, each with different coverage, costs, and provider networks. In 2026, the average Medicare beneficiary has thirty-two Medicare Advantage plans to choose from that include both medical and prescription drug coverage, according to KFF.

You can get Medicare Advantage when you first enroll in Medicare Part A and Part B, and you can enroll or switch plans during open enrollment each year, from October 15 to December 7 for new coverage starting January 1. If you already have a Medicare Advantage plan, you can also switch plans from January 1 to March 31 each year. Coverage, costs, drug formularies, and provider networks can change from year to year, so it's a good idea to compare your options each year.

ADVICE FOR CHOOSING AN ADVANTAGE PLAN

The best Medicare Advantage plan for you depends on the medication(s) you take, the doctors you use, cost sharing for your typical medical expenses, and other extra coverages you may need.

Consider the following factors whether you're enrolling for the first time or if you're comparing your options during open enrollment.

Coverage for Your Drugs

Most Medicare Advantage plans include Part D prescription drug coverage as part of the plan. Make sure the drugs you take are covered, and find out how much you'd pay out-of-pocket for them. Even though all Part D plans must limit out-of-pocket costs for prescription drugs to $2,100 in 2026, plans may charge different copayments for your medications before you hit that limit—and you won't be protected by the cap for drugs that aren't covered by your plan.

Premiums

Some Medicare Advantage plans charge a monthly premium in addition to the Part B premiums, averaging $14 per month in 2026. But two-thirds of the Medicare Advantage plans with prescription drug coverage don't charge a monthly premium, other than the Part B premium ($185 per month in 2025). Some plans also reduce the premium. However, it's important to put the premium in perspective—if a plan with a low premium doesn't cover your drugs or doctors, you may end up paying more throughout the year than you would with a plan with higher premiums.

Cost Sharing for Medical Care

Find out how much the plan charges for the types of care you use regularly, whether it's regular visits with a specialist, physical therapy, or treatment you're going through now. Compare the copayments (which is a fixed dollar amount) or coinsurance (which is a percentage of the cost) for the type of care you typically use.

Cost Sharing for Hospital Stays

The cost sharing for hospital stays is very different for a Medicare Advantage plan than it is for Original Medicare. With Original Medicare, you have to pay a Part A hospital deductible before coverage kicks in (it's $1,676 in 2025). With Medicare Advantage, you typically pay a copayment each day for the first few days—such as $460 for each of the first five days at an in-network hospital and $0 for day six and beyond. You should find out how much the plan charges for the first few days of a hospital stay, which can vary a lot by plan.

Out-of-Pocket Spending Maximum

Unlike Original Medicare, Medicare Advantage plans have an out-of-pocket spending limit for medical care (this is different from the $2,100 out-of-pocket cap for prescription drugs). In 2026, the maximum amount you have to pay for deductibles and copayments is $9,250 for in-network services and $13,900 for plans that cover both in-network and out-of-network services. Some plans offer lower limits as a way to compete. Premiums aren't included in this spending cap.

Provider Networks

If you feel strongly about seeing certain doctors, this is one of the most important factors to consider when choosing a Medicare Advantage plan. Are the doctors and hospitals you want to use covered by the plan? What happens if you use out-of-network providers?

Provider networks can change, so it's important to make sure your doctors will continue to be covered when comparing your options during open enrollment each year.

Covering Out-of-Network Providers

Some Medicare Advantage plans (typically HMOs) don't let you use any out-of-network providers except for in emergencies. Others (typically PPOs) let you use either in-network or out-of-network providers. You'll usually have lower copayments and out-of-pocket spending maximums if you use in-network providers, but you'll also have some coverage for out-of-network providers, which could make a big difference if you get diagnosed with a serious medical condition in the middle of the year.

Additional Coverage

Most Medicare Advantage plans provide coverage for some expenses that aren't included in Original Medicare, such as for dental, vision, and hearing care. But the extent of this coverage can vary a lot from plan to plan. Find out about cost sharing, maximum coverage caps, and exclusions for each kind of extra coverage before choosing a plan.

You can compare the cost and coverage for all Medicare Advantage plans in your area by using the Medicare Plan Finder (www.medicare.gov/plan-compare). You can get details about extra coverage by looking at the plan's Summary of Benefits at the insurer's website—find the links by clicking on "Plan Details" for each plan at the Plan Finder.

Star Ratings

The government rates Medicare Advantage plans based on several quality measures, with the highest being five stars. These star ratings assess plans based on customer service, complaints, how they cover chronic conditions and preventive care, and other factors. There are few five-star plans throughout the country, but if there is one in your area, you can switch into it any time of year (even outside of open enrollment). This five-star special enrollment period runs from Dec. 8 to Nov. 30 each year, and open enrollment runs from Oct. 15 to Dec. 7.

Special Coverage for Chronic Conditions

If you have a chronic condition, such as diabetes, cardiovascular disease, or end-stage renal disease, you may be eligible for a chronic condition special needs plan (C-SNP), which is a special kind of Medicare Advantage plan. The plan may have special coverage for medications and supplies related to your condition, a strong network of specialists, and a navigator to help with care coordination.

STRATEGIES FOR CHOOSING A MEDICARE ADVANTAGE PLAN

You can compare many of these features while searching for a plan in your area with the Medicare Plan Finder. Go to www.medicare.gov/plan-compare and type in your zip code, drugs, and dosages, and you'll see a list of the plans available in your area, estimated costs for your medications, and more coverage details.

SELECTING A MEDIGAP POLICY

Pick a Letter to Supplement Medicare

If you have Original Medicare and you don't have supplemental coverage from another plan, such as employer or retiree coverage, you may want to get a Medigap policy. These plans are offered by private insurers, but coverage is standardized by the federal government. There are currently ten types of plans; every policy with the same letter designation has the same coverage, although premiums may vary by insurer.

Because coverage is standardized, choosing a Medigap policy is mostly a two-step process: First, determine which letter plan you want. Then, compare premiums and pricing for the plans in your area.

You can buy any Medigap policy available in your area within six months of signing up for Medicare Part B, regardless of any preexisting conditions. You can also qualify for some Medigap policies regardless of your health in certain circumstances, such as if you move out of a Medicare Advantage plan's service area or you switch from Medicare Advantage in the first year (see www.medicare.gov/health-drug-plans/medigap/ready-to-buy for more information). If you don't qualify for any of these guaranteed issue rights, you'll also need to assess how any preexisting health conditions you have could affect your rates.

CHOOSING THE TYPE
OF MEDIGAP POLICY

In most states, there are ten types of standardized Medigap policies—identified by letters A, B, C, D, F, G, K, L, M, and N (Massachusetts, Minnesota, and Wisconsin have different options). Plans C and F are only available to people who were eligible for Medicare in 2020 or earlier, even if they didn't sign up then (new Medigap plans are no longer allowed to cover the Part B deductible). Most new Medicare enrollees can choose from eight types of policies. See www.medicare.gov/health-drug-plans/medigap/basics/compare-plan-benefits for details.

In the past, Plan F had been popular because it covered most out-of-pocket costs. New Medicare beneficiaries can no longer buy that plan, so many buy Plan G, which provides the same coverage except for the Part B deductible, which is $257 in 2025. Plan G covers the Part A deductible and hospital coinsurance, Part B 20% coinsurance, skilled nursing facility coinsurance, foreign emergency care, Part B excess charges (for doctors who won't accept assignment), and other coverage. If you want lower premiums in return for potentially larger out-of-pocket costs, you can get a high-deductible version of Plan G in some states. (High-deductible versions of Plan G have a $2,870 deductible in 2025.)

You may also have lower premiums in return for more cost sharing with plans K and L, which cover 50% or 75%, respectively, of the Part B coinsurance, Part A deductible, skilled nursing facility coverage, the hospice care copayment, and blood benefit. They have an annual out-of-pocket spending limit—$7,220 for Plan K in 2025, and $3,610 for Plan L in 2025—and the plan pays 100% of your costs for approved services after that. Plans M and N also have some cost sharing, often in return for lower premiums.

COMPARING PREMIUMS BY INSURER

After you decide which letter plan you want, compare the premiums by insurer. Remember: All plans with the same letter designation have the same coverage, even though the premiums can vary. Just like Original Medicare, Medigap plans cover any provider or facility covered by Medicare—they just supplement the Medicare coverage.

Types of Medigap Pricing

There are three types of Medigap pricing, which can affect what happens to the premiums in the future. Issue age policies base premiums on your age when you purchase the policy, attained-age policies increase premiums each year based on your rising age, and community-rated policies charge everyone the same premiums, regardless of age. All policies can increase premiums through time because of inflation. Not all options are available in every state. Make sure to find out the type of pricing for relevant plans when you compare Medigap premiums.

In some cases, premiums for attained-age policies may start out lower than issue age policies, but they might increase more through time. It can be difficult to switch policies later on, so you need to consider what may happen to premiums in the future when choosing a policy.

HOW TO COMPARE MEDIGAP OPTIONS

The Medigap insurers, policies they offer, and premiums vary by state. You can get a list of companies and policies available in your area and premium estimates with the "Find a Medigap policy that works for you" page at www.medicare.gov/medigap-supplemental-insurance-plans, and contact the company for specifics. Remember: The premiums may be different if you're not buying during a guaranteed issue period and you have any preexisting health conditions.

Your state's Department of Insurance may also be a good resource for Medigap information, as many have premium lists for the policies in their area and include information about state-specific consumer protections. You may find out, for example, whether you can buy a policy regardless of preexisting conditions at special times beyond the federal protections. You can locate your state insurance department at https://content.naic.org/state-insurance-departments. You can also get help from your local SHIP.

Spend Time Shopping for Medigap

Choose your Medigap plan carefully because it can be difficult to switch plans later. In most states, Medigap insurers can charge more or reject you because of preexisting conditions if more than six months have passed since you signed up for Medicare Part B, unless you qualify for other guaranteed issue rights (see www.medicare.gov/health-drug-plans/medigap/ready-to-buy for more information). Some states, such as Connecticut, Massachusetts, and New York, have continuous or extra guaranteed issue periods.

WHEN PREEXISTING CONDITIONS CAN AFFECT MEDIGAP PREMIUMS

The premiums listed at Medicare.gov and state insurance departments are for people who buy their Medigap policies during the six months after they sign up for Part B or a guaranteed issue period.

If you're not buying during a guaranteed issue period, you may need to answer questions about your health when you apply. Medigap insurers may charge more if you were treated or prescribed medication for certain conditions within the past two years. They may reject you if you were recently diagnosed with cancer and other conditions.

The impact of different health conditions can vary a lot by insurer. Some may offer you coverage but charge higher premiums for certain medical conditions. Others may impose a waiting period or not cover you at all.

If you're buying a Medigap policy and don't have guaranteed issue rights, it can help to work with an insurance agent who deals with several insurers' policies and knows from experience which are more likely to cover your condition at the lowest premiums. The agent can also help you gather any necessary medical records and present your case.

MOVING BETWEEN ORIGINAL MEDICARE AND MEDICARE ADVANTAGE

How to Switch Without Losing Coverage

One of the most important decisions you make after enrolling in Medicare Part A and Part B is whether you want to get your coverage from Original Medicare or a Medicare Advantage plan. That's because it can be surprisingly complicated to change your mind later.

If you have Original Medicare, it's easy to switch into Medicare Advantage—you can sign up for a Medicare Advantage plan during the annual open enrollment period, which runs from October 15 to December 7 for coverage starting January 1. Any Medicare Advantage plan in your area must accept you, regardless of your age or preexisting medical conditions (except for special needs plans that require you to have chronic or other health conditions).

You can switch from Medicare Advantage to Original Medicare during that annual open enrollment period and also during the Medicare Advantage open enrollment period from January 1 to March 31 for people who already have Medicare Advantage plans. During that January through March window, you can switch from one plan to another, or you can leave Medicare Advantage for Original Medicare.

However, switching out of Medicare Advantage can be complicated if you want to supplement Original Medicare with a Medigap policy. If you don't buy a Medigap policy at certain times, insurers in most states can reject you for coverage or charge more because of preexisting conditions. And if you have Original Medicare without some type of supplemental coverage—such as a retiree plan, TRICARE for Life, or a Medigap plan—you'll have to pay Medicare's deductibles and copayments. Plus, you may have unlimited out-of-pocket costs if you need an expensive surgery or have a long hospital stay.

When choosing between Original Medicare or Medicare Advantage in the beginning, consider your current medical expenses but also what might happen as you get older and potentially develop more medical conditions.

If you don't have many medical expenses, a Medicare Advantage plan may be less expensive than Original Medicare and Medigap, which charges higher premiums but has fewer out-of-pocket expenses. Medicare Advantage plans may have low premiums (you may not have to pay any premiums beyond the Medicare Part B premium) and if you don't have many medical expenses, you may have low out-of-pocket costs. Keep in mind that your costs may rise if you develop any health issues over the years. Medicare Advantage plans have an out-of-pocket spending maximum, but the amounts can be high compared to your budget—in 2026, the out-of-pocket spending maximum is $9,250 for covered in-network coverage and $13,900 for policies that provide in-network and out-of-network coverage. (If you have an HMO that only covers in-network care except for in emergencies, you won't have any cap on the out-of-network expenses you'd have to pay yourself.)

Keep in mind that unexpected health conditions may arise as you age, which can impact your out-of-pocket costs. For that reason, you may want to have more control over choosing your doctors and hospitals, especially if you are diagnosed with a serious condition. Original Medicare also has fewer prior authorization requirements than Medicare Advantage, although a Medicare pilot program is testing having more prior authorization requirements for Original Medicare in a few states in 2026.

It's important to think carefully about your current and future healthcare needs when you make that first decision—and to know about your options for switching to Original Medicare with a Medigap plan later on.

STRATEGIES FOR GETTING A MEDIGAP POLICY LATER ON

If you have a Medicare Advantage plan and want to switch to Original Medicare, the following strategies can help you qualify for a Medigap policy.

Medicare Advantage Trial Period

You qualify for guaranteed issue rights to get any Medigap policy if you sign up for Medicare Advantage when you're first eligible and then change your mind and switch to Original Medicare within a year. You can get any Medigap policy within that twelve-month period.

The options are slightly different if you had a Medigap policy, then dropped it to get Medicare Advantage and want to switch back to Original Medicare within twelve months. In that case, you can get the same Medigap policy you had if the insurer still offers that same policy (or more options if it isn't available anymore).

Guaranteed Issue Period If You Move Out of the Service Area

You can also qualify for a guaranteed issue period if you have Medicare Advantage and move out of the plan's service area. In that case, you can switch to Original Medicare and get almost all types of Medigap plans up to sixty days before your Medicare

Advantage coverage ends, or no more than sixty-three days afterward. (Medigap can't start until Medicare Advantage ends.)

Know Your State's Medigap Rules

A few states have very different Medigap rules. New York, Massachusetts, and Connecticut have continuous or extra open enrollment periods for Medigap, which means you can buy a policy at other times, and insurers can't charge you more or reject you because of preexisting conditions. In states with extra guaranteed issue protections, you may not need to worry as much about choosing a Medicare Advantage plan and switching to Original Medicare with a Medigap later on. Other states, such as California and Maryland, let you change from one Medigap plan to another with the same or lesser benefits around your birthday. Find out more from your local SHIP office.

IF YOU DON'T QUALIFY FOR MEDIGAP

If you don't qualify for Medigap guaranteed issue rights and can't get an affordable policy, consider making changes to your Medicare Advantage plan to provide better coverage for your needs. In cases where you have a Medicare Advantage HMO, you typically can only use doctors in the plan's provider network, and you won't have coverage for out-of-network doctors except in emergencies. If you want more flexibility to use doctors that aren't in your plan's network, consider switching from an HMO to a PPO during open enrollment in the fall. That way, you'll have some coverage for out-of-network doctors, even though you'll have to pay higher copayments than you would with in-network providers.

ANNUAL OPEN ENROLLMENT DECISIONS

Choosing Part D and Medicare Advantage Each Year

Your Part D and Medicare Advantage plan decisions don't need to be permanent. Every year, you get the opportunity to switch plans and make other coverage decisions during the annual open enrollment period, from October 15 to December 7 for new coverage starting January 1.

If you don't do anything, you can usually keep the plan you currently have. But Part D and Medicare Advantage plans can change their coverage, costs, the drugs they cover (their formularies), and their provider networks from year to year. Plus, new plans may enter the landscape and others may leave. You may have also developed different medical conditions or need new prescription drugs since you last selected your policy. Your last selection may no longer be your best option.

In addition to switching from one plan to another, you can also sign up for Part D or Medicare Advantage for the first time during open enrollment, and you can also leave Medicare Advantage for Original Medicare. (Keep in mind that you may not qualify for a Medigap policy if you have preexisting conditions, so check out those rules first.) Take advantage of open enrollment to pinpoint the best Part D or Medicare Advantage plan for you for the upcoming year.

STEPS TO TAKE DURING
OPEN ENROLLMENT

The following steps can help you choose the best Part D or Medicare Advantage plan for your needs during open enrollment.

Review the Annual Notice of Change

You'll receive this document each September from your Part D or Medicare Advantage plan. It outlines changes to the plan's coverage, costs, and networks. This will give you a heads-up about changes to your current coverage for the upcoming year.

Study the Options Available in Your Area

Even though open enrollment begins October 15, you can get a head start on your research. The Medicare.gov Plan Finder is updated with details about all of the Part D and Medicare Advantage plans available for the upcoming year around October 1. Go to the Plan Finder, type in your zip code and whether you're looking for Part D or Medicare Advantage plans, and you'll see information about every plan available in your area for the next calendar year.

Use the Plan Finder to Compare Your Options

Use the Plan Finder to compare your options for Part D or Medicare Advantage plans. Look at premiums, out-of-pocket costs, how your drugs are covered, preferred pharmacies, and star ratings. For Medicare Advantage plans, also find out whether the doctors and hospitals you want to use are included in the plan's provider network and what happens if you want to use an out-of-network provider. See the earlier entries about choosing Part D and Medicare Advantage in Chapter 1 for more details about selecting a plan.

Consider Special Needs for the Year

Think about any special medical or prescription needs you'll have for the upcoming year. If you have a Medicare Advantage plan, make sure any doctors you want to use are in the plan's provider network. If you expect to have certain procedures or surgeries, find out exactly how they're covered by the plans you're considering. If you expect to have dental procedures, for example, you may want to get a Medicare Advantage plan that offers more robust dental coverage. You can't predict everything about your health, so look at how the plan covers other things, too, such as hospital stays. Remember that you don't have to keep that plan forever—you'll have another opportunity to switch plans during open enrollment the next year.

Research Before Making Big Changes

This is also the time to consider whether you want to switch from Original Medicare to Medicare Advantage or vice versa. Keep in mind that you may have a tough time qualifying for a Medigap policy if you switch to Original Medicare and have preexisting conditions but don't qualify for Medigap guaranteed issue rights.

Sign Up for the New Plan

You have from October 15 to December 7 to sign up for a Part D or Medicare Advantage plan for the upcoming year. You can enroll in a plan using the Medicare.gov Plan Finder tool; you can also buy a plan directly from the company or from a licensed agent.

Reassess Your Medicare Advantage Plan

If you have a Medicare Advantage plan, you'll have another opportunity to switch plans from January 1 to March 31 each year. After you start to use the plan, think about whether it's doing a good job of covering your drugs and providers. If you end up getting prescribed medicines that aren't covered, discover that a preferred doctor isn't covered in the plan's provider network, or you find out your plan has a lot of prior authorization requirements, you have the first three months of the year to switch to a different Medicare Advantage plan or leave Medicare Advantage for Original Medicare. (Remember: You do not automatically qualify for a Medigap policy during this time.)

Get Help from Your State Health Insurance Assistance Program (SHIP)

Each state has its own SHIP, which provides free counseling to help with Medicare decisions, especially when choosing a Part D or Medicare Advantage plan during open enrollment each year. These experts provide one-on-one counseling and often hold seminars during open enrollment to let you know about changes in coverage and the market in your area.

You can switch Part D or Medicare Advantage plans at certain times every year: You can get a new Part D or Medicare Advantage plan or switch plans during open enrollment from October 15 to December 7 for new coverage starting January 1. If you already have a Medicare Advantage plan, you get an extra open enrollment period to switch plans or return to Original Medicare from January 1 to March 31.

But what if you want to go to a doctor who isn't in your Medicare Advantage plan's network, or you get prescribed a new drug in the middle of the year that isn't in your plan's formulary? You have limited opportunities to switch plans midyear in certain circumstances, known as special enrollment periods.

WHEN YOU CAN SWITCH PART D PLANS MIDYEAR

If you already have a Part D plan, you can switch plans outside of open enrollment in the following situations:

- If you move out of your plan's service area, you have two months to get a new Part D plan. Part D service areas usually include one state or several states, so if you move to a different state, you may be moving out of your plan's service area, depending on where you live.

- If you qualify for the Extra Help program, which provides financial assistance for Part D premiums and copayments for people with low incomes, you can switch Part D plans as much as once per month in some cases. See the Medicare Cost-Reducing Programs entry in Chapter 3 for additional resources that can help pay Medicare's costs.

- You can switch into a Part D plan with a five-star quality rating any time from December 8 to November 30 (in addition to open enrollment). However, many areas do not have a five-star plan available. Type your zip code into www.medicare.gov/plan-compare to see if there is a five-star plan in your area. The plan's star rating will be listed under each plan's name.

- You can switch Part D plans within two months of losing health insurance from your employer or union. This also includes losing COBRA coverage, which lets people who work for employers with twenty or more employees continue their employer coverage for up to eighteen months after losing their job (or thirty-six months in some situations).

- You can sign up or switch plans within two months of losing "creditable coverage," which is health insurance that is considered to be as good or better than Medicare's drug coverage.

There are also other less-common situations where you can switch Part D plans. See "Special Enrollment Periods" at Medicare.gov for details (www.medicare.gov/basics/get-started-with-medicare/get-more-coverage/joining-a-plan/special-enrollment-periods).

WHEN YOU CAN SWITCH MEDICARE ADVANTAGE PLANS MIDYEAR

You can switch from one Medicare Advantage plan to another or move from Medicare Advantage to Original Medicare in certain situations—many are similar to the Part D rules, and there are some additional situations.

- If you move out of your plan's service area, you have two months to get a new Medicare Advantage plan. If you don't choose a new plan, you'll be enrolled in Original Medicare when your Medicare Advantage plan drops you from coverage. Medicare Advantage service areas are usually much smaller than Part D service areas—they tend to be on the county rather than the state level.
- If you move to a new service area that is still covered by your plan, you also have up to two months to switch plans if new plans are available in your new service area.
- If a plan with a five-star quality rating is in your area, you can switch into that plan from December 8 to November 30, in addition to during open enrollment. However, many areas of the country do not have a five-star Medicare Advantage plan available. Type your zip code into www.medicare.gov/plan-compare to find out if there is a five-star plan in your area. Star ratings will be listed under each plan's name.
- If you're within the first twelve months of enrolling in a Medicare Advantage plan, you can drop Medicare Advantage and move into Original Medicare. You'll also have special rights to buy a Medigap policy during that time.

Get Help Switching Plans

For more information about switching Part D or Medicare Advantage plans during a special enrollment period, see "Special Enrollment Periods" at Medicare.gov. Your local SHIP can help you figure out when you can switch plans in your situation. To find out about the Part D and Medicare Advantage plans available in your area, go to www.medicare.gov/plan-compare. You can also get help by calling 1-800-MEDICARE (1-800-633-4227).

MEDICARE AND LONG-TERM CARE

How to Fill This Significant Coverage Gap

One of Medicare's biggest gaps is one of the largest expenses as many people age: long-term care. The median cost of a private room in a nursing home is more than $127,000 per year, according to the 2024 Cost of Care study by Genworth, an insurance company, and more than $70,000 for forty hours per week of home care. The median cost of one year in an assisted living facility is $70,800, and the costs can be much higher in some parts of the country.

The average person needs some level of long-term care for three years. These expenses can quickly eat through your retirement savings.

Medicare does not cover long-term care if you only need custodial care—help with activities of daily living—rather than skilled nursing care. It does cover some limited short-term care in a skilled nursing facility as rehabilitation after a qualifying hospital stay, but it doesn't cover care in a nursing home or assisted living facility for the long term. But there are other ways to help cover those potential expenses.

What Is Custodial Care?

Custodial care is help with activities of daily living, such as bathing, dressing, using the toilet, transferring, and eating. This is different from skilled care, which can include skilled nursing care, physical therapy, occupational therapy, or speech-language pathology services.

WHAT CARE EXPENSES DOES MEDICARE COVER?

Medicare does provide some short-term skilled care in limited circumstances.

Skilled Nursing Facility Care

Medicare will cover some care in a Medicare-certified skilled nursing facility as rehabilitation after a qualifying hospital stay. In most cases, you must first spend three consecutive days as an inpatient in the hospital. Time spent under observation—such as in the emergency room before you're formally admitted—doesn't count.

Your doctor must certify that you need daily skilled nursing care or physical therapy, occupational therapy, or speech-language pathology for a condition related to your hospital stay, or a new condition that started when you were in the facility.

Medicare Part A can cover up to one hundred days of skilled nursing facility care in each benefit period. Medicare covers the full cost for the first twenty days, then you pay a portion of the cost from days twenty-one to one hundred—in 2025, that copayment is $209.50. After that, you pay the full cost yourself.

You may have supplemental coverage to help with the copayment. For example, most Medigap policies cover the skilled-nursing facility copay in full or in part.

Medicare Advantage plans may have different copayments for skilled nursing facility stays.

Even though Medicare can cover up to one hundred days in a skilled-nursing facility, you're often discharged before then. It only provides coverage while you need skilled nursing care, not custo-dial care, and people are often discharged after twenty to thirty days, even if they go to a nursing home or assisted living facility after that.

Medicare and Home Care

Medicare covers home care in very specific situations: You must be homebound and need part-time or intermittent skilled nurs-ing care or therapy that is ordered by your doctor. "Homebound" means that you're unable to leave home without help from another person or a wheelchair, walker, or other special transportation. You must need the care for fewer than seven days each week or daily for fewer than eight hours a day, for up to twenty-one days. Skilled care can include skilled nursing care, physical therapy, occupational therapy, or speech-language pathology. You must be under a doctor's plan of care, and you must receive the care from a Medicare-certified home health agency. For more information, see the "Medicare & Home Health Care" booklet at Medicare.gov (www.medicare.gov/publications/10969-medicare-and-home-health-care.pdf).

HOW TO PAY FOR LONG-TERM CARE

You can get help paying for long-term custodial care from the fol-lowing sources:

Long-Term Care Insurance

You can buy long-term care insurance from a private company that will help pay for care in a nursing home, assisted living facility, or care from a home health aide. To be eligible for benefits, you usually must need help with two out of six activities of daily living—such as bathing, dressing, and eating—or your doctor must certify that you have severe cognitive impairment.

You usually buy up to a certain daily or monthly benefit amount and specify the benefit period—such as three or five years. Some older policies offered unlimited benefits, but costs have increased significantly, and new plans rarely offer unlimited benefits. The older you are when you buy the policy, the higher the premiums. Your costs are also based on your health when you buy the policy and your family health history. Insurers may reject you or charge more if you have preexisting conditions.

After years of having to pay more claims than expected, many long-term care insurance companies stopped selling new policies, so it can be more difficult to get this type of insurance than it had been in the past. It's also a lot more expensive—both for new coverage and policies purchased years ago. Because of these rising costs, some people buy just enough insurance to cover the gap between the cost of care in their area and what they could afford to pay for long-term care from their savings and income.

Hybrid Long-Term Care/Life Insurance

Hybrid policies have become more popular. They provide a death benefit if you don't need long-term care, and they can pay even more (such as three times the death benefit) if you do need long-term care. These policies tend to have the same requirements as standalone long-term care policies before they pay long-term care benefits, called benefit triggers—both types of policies generally pay benefits if you need help with two out of six activities of daily living or if there is evidence of cognitive impairment. These policies tend to be easier to qualify for than standalone long-term care insurance, but insurers still ask about your medical history.

Special Long-Term Care Benefits for Veterans

Military veterans who meet the service, asset, and income requirements to receive a veteran's pension can qualify for extra money if they need long-term care and help with activities of daily living. See "VA Aid and Attendance benefits and Housebound allowance" at VA.gov (www.va.gov/pension/aid-attendance-housebound).

Medicaid Nursing Home Benefits

If you have low assets—which can happen quickly after paying expensive long-term care costs—you may qualify for Medicaid long-term care coverage. In fact, Medicaid is the top payer of long-term care expenses. Medicaid coverage had been limited to long-term care in nursing homes, but some states now have waiver programs that let you use Medicaid to pay for assisted living or home care benefits. The rules vary by state; go to Medicaid.gov to find your state agency.

Chapter 5

Using Your Medicare Coverage

After making decisions about when to enroll in Medicare, how to get your coverage, and what supplemental plans to buy, you enroll and finally start using the coverage. But even using Medicare when you have it is not always simple: You may need to carry several insurance cards when you go to the doctor or hospital and then deal with claims for multiple policies. You may also need to navigate the prior authorization system, appeal claims denials, and search for a doctor who accepts Medicare. Or maybe you need to figure out how to get coverage for an out-of-network specialist if you have a Medicare Advantage plan. Then, if you move, you may have a limited time period to change plans.

Fortunately, there are tools and resources to help with these administrative issues. In this chapter, you'll learn about Medicare in action: how to manage your Medicare coverage in each of these situations, plus how to make the most of Medicare's free services, the benefits of setting up an online Medicare account, ways to save money on prescription drugs that aren't covered by your plan, and tax breaks for Medicare-related expenses that can help stretch your healthcare dollars.

UNDERSTANDING THE CLAIMS PROCESS

Procedures Based on Type of Coverage

Most Medicare beneficiaries have multiple policies: In addition to Medicare Part A and Part B, you may have supplemental coverage from a private Medigap plan and a separate Part D prescription drug plan. Or you could have chosen to sign up for a private Medicare Advantage plan after you enrolled in Part A and Part B.

Long story short, the insurance claims process is different for each type of coverage. Ultimately, you may need to take several insurance cards with you when you go to the doctor. This entry tells you what to expect when you start using your policies.

CLAIMS PROCESS FOR ORIGINAL MEDICARE

The process for getting medical care is usually simple if you have Original Medicare. You can use any provider who participates in the program, and you don't need a referral from your primary care physician before you can visit a specialist, so you can usually just make an appointment and go to the doctor. Just take your Medicare card to the first visit, which shows your Medicare number and when your Part A and Part B coverages started.

With Original Medicare, you typically don't need prior authorization before getting most procedures—other than prior authorization requirements for some types of durable medical equipment, nonemergency ambulance services, and some dermatology procedures to show that they are medically necessary. (Although Medicare is testing a program in a few states starting in 2026 that would expand prior authorization requirements for Original Medicare.)

If it looks like a procedure won't be covered by Medicare, your provider must have you sign an Advance Beneficiary Notice of Noncoverage (ABN) listing the items your provider thinks Medicare may not pay for, the reasons why, and the estimated cost. (However, providers aren't required to give an ABN if the service is not a Medicare benefit or is never covered.)

Your Options with a Notice of Noncoverage

If your doctor or other provider gives you an ABN alerting you that a service may not be covered by Medicare, you must choose one of three options and then sign and return the form to the doctor's office:

- You can choose to have the service anyway and pay now but have the provider submit the claim to Medicare. If Medicare does pay, the provider will refund the money. If the claim is denied, you can appeal.
- You can choose to have the service but not have the provider submit the claim to Medicare. You may have to pay for the service now, and you can't appeal because the provider didn't submit the claim.
- You don't want the service, and you don't have to make any payments. Since a claim isn't submitted to Medicare, you can't appeal.

If you didn't receive an ABN when you should have and the claim is denied, you may not be responsible for the payment. You may need to file an appeal to get the payment from the provider.

When Claims Are Automatically Submitted

If your provider participates in Medicare, then their office will submit the claim directly to Medicare. You'll receive a Medicare Summary Notice (MSN) with the status of the claim. The MSN is similar to a private insurer's Explanation of Benefits.

You rarely need to submit claims yourself. If you do, you'll submit Form CMS-1490S, "Patient's Request for Medical Payment" (available at Medicare.gov), along with an itemized bill from your provider and a letter explaining why the provider didn't submit the claim. Claims must usually be filed within twelve months after the services were provided.

Check the Status of Your Claims Quickly

You'll receive an MSN in the mail every four months for periods when you received services or medical supplies, but there are faster ways to check your claim status. You can sign up for electronic MSNs (eMSNs), and Medicare will send you a link to your MSN for any month when a claim was processed. Or you can view the status of claims within twenty-four hours of processing at your online Medicare account.

WHAT IS A MEDICARE
SUMMARY NOTICE (MSN)?

There are three types of MSNs depending on the part of Medicare that covers the service: Part A hospitalization, Part B doctors' services and outpatient care, and durable medical equipment (DME).

The MSN lists the services or supplies billed to Medicare by date, what Medicare paid, and the maximum amount you may owe. The MSN also lists how much you've paid toward the deductible for that benefit period or year and the number of benefit days used for Part A. The MSN also notes whether the claim was forwarded to your Medigap insurer or other supplemental coverage.

The last page explains how to appeal a denied claim, the deadline for appeals, and where to get help filing an appeal.

CLAIMS PROCESS FOR
SUPPLEMENTAL COVERAGE

If you have a Medigap policy, retiree plan, or other coverage to supplement Original Medicare, bring that card to your appointment too. Medicare will pay the bills first and you typically agree to have the Medigap insurer get your Part B (and sometimes Part A) claim information from Medicare.

CLAIMS PROCESS FOR MEDICARE ADVANTAGE

The claims process is different if you have a private Medicare Advantage plan. Since you need to have Medicare Part A and Part B in order to enroll in Medicare Advantage, you'll have a Medicare card in addition to a separate insurance card from your Medicare Advantage plan. Take the Medicare Advantage card to your appointment, but keep your Original Medicare card in a safe place.

Prior authorization is more common for Medicare Advantage than it is for Original Medicare. Your doctor may need to submit forms explaining why the service is medically necessary before the plan will cover it for you. Instead of an MSN, you'll receive an Explanation of Benefits listing the date of service, the provider or facility, how much of the claim was covered, what you may owe, and how to appeal.

CLAIMS PROCESS FOR PRESCRIPTION DRUG COVERAGE

If you have Original Medicare and a standalone Part D plan, you'll have a separate insurance card from the Part D company. Take that card when you go to the pharmacy. If you have drug coverage from a Medicare Advantage plan, you'll usually use the same card you used at the doctor's office.

PRIOR AUTHORIZATION AND OTHER COVERAGE RESTRICTIONS

Steps for Getting Preapproval for Claims

One of the most frustrating trends in Medicare, especially with Medicare Advantage and Part D plans, is the growing use of prior authorization. Even if your doctor prescribes a service, test, or medication that is covered by the plan, you may not be covered unless your doctor provides additional information explaining why you need that specific treatment or drug. There are also other coverage restrictions that require your doctor to jump through hoops before covering medications they've prescribed—even if the drug is covered on the plan's formulary.

The goal of these restrictions is to reduce unnecessary procedures, combat fraud, and cut back on the use of expensive drugs when a lower-cost alternative will work just as well. But the process can delay treatment and take up enormous amounts of time for providers and their office staff.

If the coverage is denied, it can be worthwhile to file an appeal or ask for an exception—a large percentage of these restrictions are overturned at the next step. This entry will explain how to deal with these restrictions and get the coverage you need.

PRIOR AUTHORIZATION

Prior authorization requires your doctor to submit information explaining why you need a treatment or medication, even if it is covered by Medicare or your plan. Prior authorization requirements and procedures can be different based on the type of coverage you have. They're much more common in Medicare Advantage and Part D than they are in Original Medicare.

Prior Authorization for Medicare Advantage

Prior authorization is most common for Medicare Advantage plans—99% of plans require prior authorization before covering some services, according to KFF. And the use of prior authorization is growing: Medicare Advantage insurers made nearly 50 million prior authorization determinations in 2023, up from 37 million in 2021.

Services Most Frequently Requiring Prior Authorization

In 2025, Medicare Advantage plans most commonly require prior authorization for durable medical equipment, skilled nursing facility stays, Part B drugs, acute inpatient hospital stays, psychiatric hospital stays, diagnostic procedures and tests, and home health services, according to KFF.

Work with your doctor to get the prior authorization forms submitted and to appeal if the request is denied. In 2023, Medicare Advantage insurers fully or partially denied 3.2 million requests for prior authorization. Fewer than 12% of those denials were appealed, but more than 81% of the appeals were partially or fully overturned, according to KFF.

Prior Authorization for Original Medicare

Original Medicare has very few prior authorization requirements. Your doctor rarely needs to submit extra forms before a service will be covered. Original Medicare's prior authorization requirements are generally related to:

- **Durable medical equipment:** Medicare requires prior authorization for a long list of durable medical equipment to try to reduce fraud. For example, your provider may need to submit extra forms explaining why you need certain kinds of power wheelchairs and hospital beds.
- **Nonemergency ambulance services:** Medicare covers emergency ambulance services and sometimes pays for an ambulance when it is not an emergency if it is medically necessary because other types of transportation could endanger your health.
- **Certain outpatient services:** Medicare requires providers to submit extra information showing that some procedures are medically necessary and should be covered, rather than just cosmetic and not covered—such as rhinoplasty (nose job) and blepharoplasty (eyelid surgery).

The Centers for Medicare & Medicaid Services announced that it will run a pilot program starting in 2026 with additional prior authorization requirements for Original Medicare in six states. This program focuses on certain kinds of procedures, such as knee arthroscopy for knee osteoarthritis and electrical nerve stimulator implants. For more information, see the WISeR (Wasteful and Inappropriate Service Reduction) Model fact sheets at www.cms.gov.

Prior Authorization for Part D Prescription Drug Plans

Even if a drug is covered on a Part D plan's formulary, your doctor or other prescriber may need to provide extra information before your plan will cover the prescription for you. Sometimes plans require prior authorization because a drug is only approved in certain circumstances. For example, Medicare is not allowed to cover drugs prescribed specifically for weight loss. Ozempic is included on most Part D plans' formularies for people with type 2 diabetes who meet the FDA requirements. It's not covered when prescribed specifically for weight loss.

Your doctor may need to submit prior authorization forms explaining why an expensive specialty drug is medically necessary before it will be covered.

OTHER COVERAGE RESTRICTIONS FOR PRESCRIPTION DRUGS

Part D plans and Medicare Advantage plans with prescription drug coverage may also have two other kinds of coverage restrictions before you can use certain drugs on their formularies: step therapy and quantity limits.

With step therapy, you have to try a less expensive drug that has been found to be effective for people with your condition before the plan will cover the more expensive medication. Your prescriber can ask for an exception by explaining why you need the more expensive drug—for example, if you've had a reaction to the other medication, or if it will be less effective for you.

With quantity limits, the plan will only cover a certain dosage or number of tablets each month. Your prescriber can ask for an exception by explaining why it's medically necessary for you to have the higher dose.

APPEALING COVERAGE DENIALS

Perseverance Can Pay Off

If Medicare or a Medicare Advantage plan refuses to pay for a treatment—either at the prior authorization level or after the fact—you have several levels of appeal and resources that can help. The process is different depending on the type of plan that you have.

APPEALING AN ORIGINAL MEDICARE CLAIM DENIAL

Original Medicare typically has a few situations where it requires prior authorization. For example, you or your doctor may need to submit extra paperwork before you can receive coverage for dermatology that could be considered cosmetic, proving nonemergency ambulance services were necessary for your health, and proving durable medical equipment is medically necessary (not fraudulent). Your doctor can usually submit information explaining why you need the procedure, ambulance services, or equipment to help get the prior authorization denial reversed.

If a claim is denied after the service is provided, first contact your provider and ask for an itemized bill. There may have been charges for services you didn't receive or coding errors that caused the claim to be denied by Medicare. Or they may not have sent the bill to your supplemental insurer, leaving you with charges for deductibles and copayments you may not need to pay.

Next, review the MSN, which lists the services, dates, and providers or facilities; whether the claim was approved; and the amount of non-covered charges. The last page details information on appealing denied claims, including the specific deadline for submitting the appeal to Medicare (120 days after receiving the notice).

You can use the MSN to file the first level of appeal. Circle the services you disagree with, attach an explanation about why you disagree with the decision, and add additional information to support your case. Your provider's office can help you provide information showing why the service was medically necessary. Then, submit the notice and supporting documents to the Medicare claims office listed on the form. You'll generally get a decision from the Medicare Administrative Contractor within sixty days after receiving the appeal. If that appeal is denied, you have several more levels of appeal you can go through.

You have 180 days after that decision to request the next level of appeal: a reconsideration by a Qualified Independent Contractor (QIC), an independent entity who was not involved in the original decision. You can include additional documentation to strengthen your case. You'll usually receive a decision within sixty days after the QIC receives your request, and then you have sixty days from the date of the QIC decision to appeal to the next level if denied.

The third level of appeal is a hearing in front of an administrative law judge, which is only available for claims worth $190 or more in 2025. The hearing is generally held by phone or video conference, where you (or a lawyer representing you) have an opportunity to present your case.

There are two more levels of appeals, which are rare and usually have long waiting periods—review by the Medicare Appeals Council and judicial review in Federal District Court. See "Appeals in Original Medicare" at Medicare.gov for details about each level of appeal and the time frames.

Getting Help with an Appeal

Your doctor's office may be helpful with the appeal. Their staff is familiar with the coverage issues and may have experience appealing similar denials. You can also get help from your local SHIP or the Center for Medicare Advocacy, whose website is filled with resources for appeals. You can also learn from other people's experiences through advocacy groups specializing in your condition.

APPEALING A MEDICARE ADVANTAGE CLAIM DENIAL

The first few time frames and steps are different for Medicare Advantage denials. Work with your provider to appeal a prior authorization request—some doctor's offices have dedicated staff members focusing on prior authorization. The provider may be able to participate in a peer-to-peer review, where they can talk with a physician at the insurance company about why the service is medically necessary.

For denials after you have received the service (rather than prior authorization denials), you'll receive an Explanation of Benefits (EOB) from your Medicare Advantage plan each month you receive a service, visit a provider, or fill a prescription. The document shows the date of service, description, whether or not the claim was paid, what was paid by the insurer, and what you owe.

If you disagree with the claim decision, first contact your provider to make sure it wasn't just an error. If that doesn't help, you can appeal—the EOB includes the steps for appealing. You have just sixty-five days, rather than 120 days, to submit the first level of appeal for a Medicare Advantage plan. The appeal must be decided within sixty days for payment appeals (after the service is provided) or thirty days for pre-service appeals. If that appeal is denied, it's automatically sent to the next level of appeal, which is an Independent Review Entity.

The next steps are the same as they are with Original Medicare: a hearing with an administrative law judge, followed by the Medicare Appeals Council, and Federal District Court. For more information, see "Appeals in Medicare health plans" at Medicare.gov.

APPEALING A PART D CLAIM DENIAL

Part D denials are different because you usually discover that the drug isn't covered at the pharmacy counter. Your plan may not cover the drug because it's not on the plan's formulary or you haven't received prior authorization. Ask the plan why coverage was denied and if there's anything your provider can do—either submitting prior authorization forms or asking if they can prescribe a similar drug that is covered by your plan.

If you can't switch to another drug, file an exception request with your plan, with supporting documents from your prescriber. You can ask for an expedited decision if waiting could jeopardize your health.

If the exception is denied, you can start the formal appeals process. See "Appeals in a Medicare drug plan" at Medicare.gov for the procedure and time frame to appeal.

FINDING A DOCTOR WHO ACCEPTS MEDICARE

Not Every Doctor Accepts New Patients

If you have Original Medicare, you don't need to worry about provider networks: You can use any doctor throughout the United States who accepts Medicare, and the vast majority of doctors participate in the program. However, there are some specialties where it can be more difficult to find doctors who accept Medicare, and some doctors who participate in Medicare aren't accepting new patients.

In 2024, only 1.2% of physicians who aren't pediatricians opted out of the Medicare program, according to a study by KFF. But the percentages are larger for some specialties—for example, 8.1% of psychiatrists, 4.5% of plastic surgeons, and 3.2% of physicians specializing in neurology opted out of Medicare. The opt-out rates are higher in some states.

You can find doctors who participate in the Medicare program by visiting www.medicare.gov/care-compare and clicking on "Doctors & clinicians." Enter your zip code and the type of provider you're looking for. If the doctor accepts assignment, which means they accept Medicare's payment in full, there will be a note that says, "Charges the Medicare-approved amount (so you pay less out-of-pocket)."

If the doctor does not accept assignment, they may be able to charge up to 15% more than the Medicare-approved amount. (This is known as balance billing; it is not permitted in some states, such as Ohio.) You'll have to pay this 15% in addition to the 20% Part B coinsurance. Medigap Plan F and Plan G cover the 15% Part B excess charge in addition to the 20% Part B coinsurance.

Just because a doctor is participating in Medicare doesn't mean that they are accepting new patients, so you may need to make several calls. A 2022 study by KFF found that only 83% of primary care physicians were accepting new Medicare patients, and only 60% of psychiatrists were accepting new Medicare patients.

Another option for primary care is to work with a nurse practitioner or physician's assistant who is in a primary care practice, or to pay a monthly subscription fee for concierge care. With this type of care, you pay a monthly fee to have access to the doctor or practice and may receive enhanced services. For psychiatrists, you may have more options if you pay out of your pocket for the visits.

DIRECT PRIMARY CARE AND NEW HSA RULES

A growing number of doctors have been switching to a subscription-based concierge care or direct primary care model. Rather than using insurance, you pay a monthly fee for primary care services. According to a study by Grand View Research, the concierge medicine market is expected to grow by more than 10% per year from 2025 to 2030. This is one way to find a doctor who is accepting new patients. Medicare doesn't cover the subscription fee, but if the doctor participates in Medicare, the rest of their services will be covered as other doctor's services.

A new rule can help make this subscription strategy a bit more affordable for people with money in health savings accounts

(HSAs). Starting in 2026, people who have saved money in a health savings account can withdraw money tax-free from an HSA to pay direct primary care fees of up to $150 per month for individuals or $300 for families.

You can't make new contributions to an HSA after you've enrolled in Medicare, but if you already have money in an HSA, taking tax-free withdrawals for this eligible expense can help you afford this model of care. Not all concierge care providers qualify—their practice must be limited to primary care, and the monthly fee cannot be more than $150 per month for individuals or $300 for families.

DOCTORS WHO OPT OUT OF MEDICARE

Even though just over 1% of non-pediatric doctors don't participate in Medicare, you may have a harder time finding certain kinds of doctors: A larger percentage of psychiatrists, plastic surgeons, and neurologists have opted out of Medicare, and not all concierge doctors participate in Medicare.

If you work with a doctor who doesn't participate in Medicare, the claim procedures and payment rules are totally different. These doctors can't bill Medicare for services you receive, and they don't have to accept Medicare's payment amount—or even the 15% over the Medicare-approved amount for doctors who don't accept assignment. Instead, you enter into your own contract with the provider and agree to pay their bill in full. There's no limit as to how much they can charge. If they don't participate in Medicare, then a Medigap plan won't cover the charges, either.

Different Rules for Medicare Advantage Plans

Finding a new doctor can be more complicated in Medicare Advantage plans, which have limited provider networks. Before you decide between Original Medicare and Medicare Advantage, consider the availability of doctors in your area. Look at the provider lists on the Medicare Advantage plan's website to see which doctors and facilities are covered, even for specialties you don't need yet. Some plans with the lowest premiums (or no premiums) have narrow networks and fewer options.

GET COVERAGE FOR OUT-OF-NETWORK DOCTORS

Specialists Not in Your Plan

If you have a Medicare Advantage plan, one of the most important steps you can take during open enrollment each year is to make sure the doctors you want to use are still covered in the plan's provider network. It is becoming easier to access this information through the Medicare.gov Plan Finder tool, and you can also check the provider database on the plan's website (see the link in the Plan Finder).

If you like your current doctors, ask whether they'll participate in the plan next year, and be sure to mention your specific plan—some Medicare Advantage insurers offer several plans in an area, each with different provider networks. Also, make sure to check on doctors and specialists you use regularly, and find out whether your preferred hospitals are covered by the plan's network.

GETTING COVERAGE FOR OUT-OF-NETWORK DOCTORS MIDYEAR

You'll have fewer options if you are diagnosed with a serious disease midyear and you want to use an expert specialist for treating your condition. If that doctor isn't included in your Medicare Advantage plan's provider network, you'll have limited options for getting coverage. But before you give up on seeing them or drain your retirement savings to pay their bills, give the following strategies a try:

Ask for a Network Exception

If a doctor you want to use isn't covered and you can prove that no one in your plan's network can do the necessary type of specialty care you need, you may get coverage under a network exception. You need to build a compelling case that your current plan doesn't include an in-network specialist who provides the specialized care, and your doctor's office may be able to help. The procedures for requesting a network exception vary by insurer. If you do get approval to use the out-of-network provider, get it in writing in case they try to deny the claim later.

Consider Switching to Original Medicare

If you have Original Medicare rather than a Medicare Advantage plan, you can use any doctor who participates in the program, and you don't need a referral—that is one of the biggest benefits to Original Medicare. By switching from Medicare Advantage to Original Medicare, you could get coverage for the doctor you prefer. It's easy to make the change during open enrollment (October 15 to December 7 for new coverage starting January 1) or during the annual Medicare Advantage open enrollment period (January 1 to March 31 with new coverage starting the next month). However, you may have a tough time getting a Medigap plan to help pay for your out-of-pocket expenses for Original Medicare.

Without Medigap, you could have to pay the Part A hospital deductible and coinsurance yourself and the 20% Part B coinsurance—which can add up quickly if you need expensive specialty care.

If more than six months have passed since you signed up for Medicare Part B, Medigap insurers in most states can deny coverage or charge you more because of preexisting conditions. However, a few states have special rules allowing you to get a Medigap policy regardless of health issues at any time. In that case, it's much easier to switch from Medicare Advantage back to Original Medicare. Contact your SHIP program to learn about your state's rules and for help with your options.

Switch to a Medicare Advantage PPO

If none of the Medicare Advantage plans in your area cover the specialist you want to use, you could switch to another Medicare Advantage plan that provides some out-of-network coverage. A Medicare Advantage HMO usually doesn't cover out-of-network care except for emergencies, while a Medicare Advantage PPO usually covers both in-network and out-of-network care. Keep in mind that with this out-of-network option, you'll have to pay higher copayments or coinsurance for the out-of-network providers, and you will have a higher out-of-pocket spending cap—up to $9,250 in 2026 for in-network care and $13,900 for plans that provide in-network and out-of-network care, although some plans have lower caps. After you reach that cap, the plan must pay the rest of the covered costs for the year.

Find Out If You Can Switch Plans Midyear

You may not have to wait until open enrollment to switch plans. If you already have Medicare Advantage, you can also switch plans from January 1 to March 31 with new coverage starting the next month. If a Medicare Advantage plan in your area has a five-star quality rating, you can switch into that plan from December 8 to November 30, in addition to the open enrollment period (check the Medicare Plan Finder). See the entry Changing Coverage Midyear in Chapter 4 for more options.

FREE BENEFITS OF MEDICARE

Preventive Care and Wellness Programs Without Copays

Even though Medicare can cover most of your medical expenses after you turn sixty-five, you usually have to pay deductibles and copayments, including 20% of the cost of doctors' services and outpatient care. However, there are several things that Medicare gives you for no additional cost—mostly preventive care with the goal of helping to detect health issues early, before they become more expensive diseases.

The Affordable Care Act made a lot of preventive care free from any out-of-pocket costs, and the Inflation Reduction Act expanded the list. Eligibility for these services is usually based on age, risk factors, and time frame. Search for "Preventive and screening services" at Medicare.gov for a full list and criteria. You can keep track of preventive services you're eligible for at your online Medicare account. The following are some services that Medicare covers for free.

VACCINES

The Affordable Care Act made vaccines covered by Medicare Part B free starting in 2011. But some vaccines are covered by Part D prescription drug coverage rather than Part B, such as the shingles vaccine. Until recently, those vaccines were still subject to deductibles and copayments. The Inflation Reduction Act of 2022 changed the rules; since January 2023, all adult vaccines recommended by the Centers for Disease Control and Prevention's Advisory Committee on Immunization Practices are covered with no out-of-pocket costs, whether they're covered by Part B or Part D. Eligibility can be based on age, risk factors, and time of year.

Medicare Part B covers an annual flu vaccine, hepatitis B for people who are medium or high risk, pneumonia, and certain COVID-19 vaccines without any cost sharing.

Medicare Part D covers the vaccine for hepatitis A, hepatitis B for people at high risk, respiratory syncytial virus (RSV), shingles, Tdap, and others.

If you have a Medicare Advantage plan with drug coverage, it must also cover the Part B and Part D vaccines without any out-of-pocket costs. You may need to use an in-network provider.

SCREENINGS AND TESTS

Medicare Part B covers many screenings and tests without any cost sharing, including screenings for colorectal cancer, prostate cancer, lung cancer, cervical cancer, and mammograms to detect breast cancer. Eligibility is usually based on age and risk factors. It also covers up to two diabetes screenings each year if you're at risk of developing diabetes.

Part B also covers screening for alcohol misuse and up to four counseling sessions per year, annual depression screening through your primary care doctor, and screening for sexually transmitted infections.

WELLNESS PROGRAMS AND COUNSELING

Medicare Part B covers wellness programs and counseling for people at risk for certain conditions, including a year-long diabetes prevention program for people with certain body mass index (BMI) and blood sugar levels, medical nutrition therapy services for people with diabetes or kidney disease, and obesity behavioral therapy for people with a BMI of 30 or higher. Part B can also cover up to eight sessions of smoking cessation counseling during a twelve-month period.

"WELCOME TO MEDICARE" VISIT

You can get this "Welcome to Medicare" visit any time within the first twelve months of enrolling in Medicare Part B. The doctor or other provider will review your medical history, calculate your BMI, assess your potential risk factors, screen for depression, give you a simple vision test, let you know about other screenings and preventive services, and talk about advance directives.

It's a good opportunity to meet with the provider and set a baseline for future visits, especially if you start going to a new doctor after you sign up for Medicare. Note that while this "Welcome to Medicare" session has no additional cost, you may have to pay the Part B deductible and 20% coinsurance if your doctor provides other services or performs additional tests during or after this session.

YEARLY WELLNESS VISIT

Medicare Part B covers a wellness visit with your primary care provider every twelve months after you've been enrolled for a year. (Having the "Welcome to Medicare" visit is not a prerequisite for these annual visits, although it can be helpful.) The provider will measure your height, weight, and blood pressure; perform a cognitive assessment; review your medical history and risk factors; and focus on creating a personalized prevention plan. The provider can also review your current medications, which can help to make sure your prescriptions from different specialists are coordinated.

Medicare Doesn't Cover a Physical Exam

The "Welcome to Medicare" and the yearly wellness visits are different from a physical exam, which isn't covered by Original Medicare. These wellness visits focus on assessing risk factors and creating a personalized prevention plan. An annual physical exam usually includes blood and urine tests, measures your blood pressure and heart rate, and includes a hands-on assessment from your physician. Physical exams may have been covered by your employer or individual health insurance before enrolling in Medicare, and some Medicare Advantage plans include them, but they are not covered by Original Medicare.

HOW RELOCATING CAN AFFECT MEDICARE

Different Procedures Based on Type of Coverage

Original Medicare covers any doctor who participates in the program throughout the country, so your coverage won't change if you move within the United States. However, you may need to make changes to your other coverage, and you will need to change plans if you have Medicare Advantage or Part D and you move outside of the plan's service area. And moving may qualify you for special enrollment periods to reassess the type of coverage you have. Here are the steps you need to take if you move.

ORIGINAL MEDICARE WHEN YOU MOVE

Even though your Original Medicare coverage won't change when you move, you should still update your address with Medicare so you can get your Medicare Summary Notices (MSNs), annual "Medicare & You" handbook, and other statements.

To update your address for Medicare, go to the Social Security Administration website and log on to your *my* Social Security account (Social Security handles a lot of administrative issues for Medicare). You can also call the Social Security Administration at 1-800-772-1213 or visit a local office.

To update your phone number and email address, go to Medicare.gov and click on "Log in" to sign in or create an account.

If you move to a foreign country, your Medicare coverage won't work while you're abroad, but you can keep the coverage and pay Part B premiums (and Part A premiums if you aren't eligible for premium-free Part A). If you don't keep your Part B and you don't have health insurance from your employer or from a national health system or volunteer organization that provides health insurance, you may need to pay a late enrollment penalty if you sign up for coverage after you return. You have an eight-month special enrollment period to get coverage after you stop working, or six months if you had coverage while volunteering.

MEDIGAP WHEN YOU MOVE

If you have a Medigap policy to supplement Original Medicare, Medigap covers its share of bills after Original Medicare pays out. You can use any doctor or hospital throughout the United States that accepts Medicare.

You usually aren't required to switch Medigap plans if you move, but you should let your insurer know. They may let you keep your rate in the state where you originally lived, or they may change your rates based on the new area.

Medigap plans are regulated by states rather than the federal government, so you may have some new consumer protections after you've relocated. In New York, Massachusetts, and Connecticut, for example, you can buy a Medigap policy any time even if you have health issues. In other states, Medigap insurers can reject you or charge more because of preexisting conditions, unless you buy a policy during certain times—such as the six months after signing up for Medicare Part B.

PART D PRESCRIPTION DRUG COVERAGE WHEN YOU MOVE

You may be moving out of your Part D plan's service area if you move to a new state. If you move out of your Part D plan's service area, you typically have a two-month special enrollment period to get another Part D plan. If you don't notify the plan of your move, the insurer can drop you from coverage if it discovers you have a new address outside of its service area. Even before then, you might have a hard time finding preferred pharmacies after you move.

The length of your special enrollment period depends on when you let the plan know that you're moving. If you notify your plan before you move, the special enrollment period begins the month before you move and lasts for two months after you move. Otherwise, your special enrollment period lasts for two months after you move.

MEDICARE ADVANTAGE WHEN YOU MOVE

The service areas for Medicare Advantage plans are smaller than they are for standalone Part D plans. Medicare Advantage plans often serve a city or a county rather than a whole state, so even moving across town could land you in a new service area.

You typically have two months after moving outside of the Medicare Advantage plan's service area to get a new plan. But it's better not to wait: It may be hard to find in-network providers and preferred pharmacies after you move. You can be dropped from coverage if you don't notify the plan that you moved outside of its service area.

You can also qualify for a special enrollment period to get a new plan if you move within the plan's service area, but there are different plan options available in your new area.

If you don't like your new Medicare Advantage options after you move, you also have the option to switch to Original Medicare and qualify for a Medigap plan with guaranteed issue protections.

An Extra Chance to Qualify for Medigap

If you have Medicare Advantage and are moving outside of the plan's service area, it's also a good opportunity to reassess how you want to get your coverage—especially if your healthcare expenses have increased or you no longer want to be limited to in-network providers. When moving, you can switch to Original Medicare and qualify for a Medigap policy regardless of preexisting conditions. You'll have guaranteed issue rights to get most Medigap policies if you apply sixty days before your Medicare Advantage plan ends or up to sixty-three days after it ends.

CAPITALIZING ON YOUR ONLINE MEDICARE ACCOUNT

The Easiest Way to Manage Medicare Information

An online Medicare account can help you manage your Medicare coverage and access important resources. You'll be able to review claims within twenty-four hours of processing, rather than waiting for a paper report in the mail every four months. You can print out an official Medicare card any time, learn about preventive care you're eligible for, save information about your prescription drugs to make it easier to shop for Part D or Medicare Advantage plans, and pay your premiums online.

The following will teach you how to set up an online Medicare account and how to make the most of this resource.

HOW TO SET UP AN ONLINE MEDICARE ACCOUNT

Go to Medicare.gov, click on "Log in" and then either sign in to your account with your username and password or click on "Create Account with Medicare.gov." Type in your Medicare number and your Part A start date, which you can find on your Medicare card, and some additional personal information. If you don't have your Medicare card, you can get the information by logging on to your *my* Social Security account (you can create that account at the Social Security Administration website).

REVIEW CLAIMS QUICKLY

Medicare mails beneficiaries a Medicare Summary Notice (MSN) every four months when they have claims, but you can get the information much faster through your online Medicare account. You can sign up for electronic MSNs and then receive an email with your MSNs every month you have claims. You'll receive separate MSNs for Part A, Part B, and durable medical equipment claims.

Even better, you can review your Medicare claims in your online account within twenty-four hours of processing, which can be a great way to know what to expect to pay, spot any errors, and get clues of potential fraud. These notices also include the time frame and steps for appealing claim denials.

Please note that this claims information is only for Original Medicare. You'll get a separate Explanation of Benefits for Medicare Advantage claims.

PAY YOUR MEDICARE PREMIUMS

Most people have their Medicare premiums automatically deducted from their Social Security benefits. But if you haven't signed up for Social Security benefits yet, you have other options: You can go to your online Medicare account and sign up to have Medicare premiums withdrawn automatically from your bank account through the Medicare Easy Pay program, or you can pay the bills electronically through your online Medicare account.

Most people don't have to pay premiums for Part A because they (or their spouse) paid Medicare taxes from their paychecks for at least ten years. But you do have to pay monthly Part B premiums, and people with high incomes have to pay even more if they are subject to the Income-Related Monthly Adjustment Amount (IRMAA). You can pay your Part B premiums and IRMAA and your Part D IRMAA on your online Medicare account. You can also pay Part A premiums there if you have them. Your options are different if you get your Medicare bills from the Railroad Retirement Board.

REPLACE YOUR MEDICARE CARD

If you lose your Medicare card, you don't have to wait for the Social Security Administration to mail you a new one. Instead, you can print it out from your online Medicare account. That version is just as official as ordering a card through the mail.

KEEP TRACK OF PRESCRIPTION DRUGS

You can also keep track of the prescription drugs and pharmacies you use on your online Medicare account, which can give you a head start when you're comparing plans during open enrollment in the fall. While online, you can see a list of prescriptions you've filled in the past twelve months.

Use the Medicare Plan Finder to compare all of the Part D and Medicare Advantage options in your area during open enrollment. While doing that, log on to your online Medicare account and use your saved drugs and pharmacies to see how much the plans would charge for your specific drugs and dosages without having to type them into the tool separately.

OTHER BENEFITS

Your online Medicare account can also give you a total summary of the Medicare coverage you currently have, and a list of preventive benefits that are available to you. Most are free from any out-of-pocket costs. Finally, you can access resources, such as the "Medicare & You" handbook, which Medicare sends before open enrollment every year. This booklet contains detailed information about Medicare's coverage and costs for the upcoming year and is a great resource.

Separate Resources for Supplemental Policies

If you have a Medicare Advantage plan, Part D prescription drug coverage, or a Medigap plan, you'll need to go to each of those insurers' websites separately to find out about online resources. You may be able to sign up to access claims information online soon after the claims are processed, review information about your coverage, and find out about in-network doctors and covered drugs. So, make sure to sign up for these resources.

SAVING MONEY ON PRESCRIPTION DRUGS

Options If Your Drugs Aren't Covered

Medicare beneficiaries with prescription drug coverage from a standalone Part D plan or a Medicare Advantage plan don't need to worry about open-ended drug costs. Starting in 2025, both plans cap out-of-pocket spending on covered drugs (the cap was $2,000 in 2025 and rose to $2,100 for inflation in 2026). That includes deductibles (which can be up to $615 for Part D plans in 2026) and copayments (your share of the cost of the drugs), but not premiums. Once you reach that limit, your drugs are covered by your plan for the rest of the year. The US Department of Health and Human Services estimated that about 11.3 million Part D enrollees would reach the cap in 2025.

That said, the drugs still must be included in your plan's formulary—its list of covered drugs—to be subject to the cap. Not all plans cover all drugs, and the formulary lists can change from year to year. If your drug isn't covered by the plan, not only will you have to pay the cost yourself, but those costs won't count toward the $2,100 cap.

If your doctor prescribes a drug that isn't covered by your plan, you have a few options—either for trying to get coverage or for assistance with the drug costs. The following are some avenues to try.

ASK YOUR DOCTOR ABOUT THERAPEUTIC ALTERNATIVES

Before you leave the doctor's office with a prescription, look up the drug on the Medicare Plan Finder or your plan's website to find out whether it's covered. If not, ask your doctor about therapeutic alternatives, which are other drugs that meet the same need but may be less expensive or covered by your plan. These alternatives can be generic medications or other brand-name drugs. You can also ask your pharmacist for alternatives to talk with your doctor about.

USE COUPONS FROM COST-SAVING WEBSITES

Several websites, such as GoodRx.com, provide coupons you can present to the pharmacist for discounts on prescription drugs. However, you can't use these coupons with Medicare coverage. If the price with the coupon is less than the copay with prescription drug coverage, some people use cash with the coupon instead. But the strategy is different now that Part D has a $2,100 cap on out-of-pocket spending. In that case, it may be better to use your insurance instead—even if it costs slightly more—so your cost counts toward the cap, if it looks like you'll get close to reaching the $2,100 cap before year-end.

If the drug isn't covered by your plan's formulary, using the coupon can help bring down the cost you'd have to pay with cash anyway.

FIND A LOWER-COST PHARMACY

Prescription drug prices can vary a lot depending on where you buy the medication. If the drug isn't on your plan's formulary, shop around at a few pharmacies in your area—GoodRx.com is also a good resource to compare costs at local pharmacies.

If the drug is covered by Part D, the plan usually has preferred pharmacies that charge lower copayments—you can use the Medicare Plan Finder to search for preferred pharmacies in your area for each plan.

RE-SHOP YOUR PART D OR MEDICARE ADVANTAGE PLAN

You have the opportunity to switch Part D and Medicare Advantage plans each year during open enrollment. You have from October 15 to December 7 each year to choose a new plan with coverage starting January 1. People with Medicare Advantage plans also have from January 1 to March 31 to switch to a different plan. If your doctor prescribes a new medication midyear that isn't covered by your plan, you may have to pay the cost yourself for a few months before you have an opportunity to switch plans. Go to the Medicare.gov Plan Finder, and type in the drug and dosage to find out how each plan in your area covers the drug.

You may also be able to switch into a Part D or Medicare Advantage plan with a five-star quality rating outside of open enrollment, if one is available in your area. Before you switch, find out how the plan covers your other medications and, if you have a Medicare Advantage plan, how it covers your doctors and other healthcare needs.

ASK FOR A FORMULARY EXCEPTION

Your doctor or other prescriber can ask your Part D plan for a formulary exception if another drug can't fill the same need for you or if your plan stops covering your drug. Have your doctor provide evidence about why you need that particular medication rather than any alternatives that are covered by your plan.

HELP FROM FOUNDATIONS FOCUSING ON YOUR CONDITION

Several nonprofit organizations provide resources to help pay prescription drug costs for people with certain diseases. Some are only available to people below a certain income level, but cutoffs can be high. You can search for assistance at the Patient Advocate Foundation (www.patientadvocate.org) and the PAN Foundation (www.panfoundation.org).

Resources from Disease-Specific Organizations

You can find out about special programs to help with drug costs and other coverage issues for people with a similar diagnosis through disease-specific organizations, such as the American Cancer Society, Susan G. Komen for breast cancer, American Diabetes Association, American Heart Association, and American Kidney Fund. Many of these organizations also have guides to navigating Medicare and finding resources that can help you pay for care and medications.

PHARMACEUTICAL
ASSISTANCE PROGRAMS

Drug manufacturers often have pharmaceutical assistance programs to help with the cost of their medications if you don't have coverage from your insurance. You can search for these assistance plans based on your drug with the "Find a Pharmaceutical Assistance Program for the drugs you take" search tool at Medicare.gov. State Pharmaceutical Assistance Programs can also help with the costs. These programs may be available to people below certain income levels or with certain diseases. To check if your state has a program, use the "Find out if your state has a State Pharmaceutical Assistance Program" search tool at Medicare.gov, or ask your State Health Insurance Assistance Program (SHIP) about the state pharmaceutical assistance search and other programs in the area.

AVOIDING MEDICARE SCAMS

Check Claims Notices for Suspicious Charges

Medicare scams are big business: The program loses about $60 billion each year to fraud, errors, and abuse (such as billing for more expensive services than were actually performed). It's easy for thieves to steal money from Medicare because you may never receive a bill if you have a supplemental policy. The crooks can inflate charges, double bill, or make up fake claims, and you may have no idea it's happening unless you review your Medicare Summary Notice. Or they may use impostor scams, preying upon your concern about losing valuable government benefits as a way to steal your personal information, money, and identity.

Here are several Medicare-related scams to watch out for, what you can do to protect yourself, and where to report suspected fraud.

FAKE CLAIMS USING YOUR MEDICARE NUMBER

Thieves can steal your Medicare number—or trick you into giving it out—and then use it to file fake claims in your name. Sometimes they offer to send equipment, like knee braces, then give you a flimsy version while billing Medicare for a fancy one. Or they'll file claims for doctors you never saw or equipment you never received. They've even signed up people who aren't terminally ill for hospice without their knowing—until the Medicare beneficiary tries to use

Medicare to pay for regular medical charges, which are no longer covered once they're on hospice.

Don't ever give your Medicare number to anyone except to a doctor or provider. Review your MSN for suspicious activity—the notice lists the service and date, so it can be easy to detect charges for services you never received. You'll receive these statements in the mail every four months that you have a claim, or you can access them at your online Medicare account within twenty-four hours after the claim is processed.

MEDICARE CARD SCAMS

Medicare card scams were a big problem in 2018 when Medicare first introduced new cards with eleven-digit alphanumeric numbers instead of using Social Security numbers. The change was designed to help protect Medicare beneficiaries from identity theft, but the transition ended up leading to a new group of scams: Thieves would call Medicare beneficiaries and ask for their personal information—including their Social Security number—which they claimed they needed to send out the new card.

Those scams became popular again recently, as thieves called claiming to be a Medicare representative offering a plastic card with a chip. They'd ask for money for the new card or for your Medicare number to send it out.

Please remember: Medicare won't call you about a new card and the company does not offer plastic cards or cards with chips. Medicare will never call to ask for your Social Security number or Medicare number. You can print out an official card from your online Medicare account.

MEDICARE FLEX CARD SCAMS

Medicare flex cards are offered by Medicare Advantage plans to help pay out-of-pocket costs, over-the-counter medicine, dental copays, and other expenses. However, scammers have been calling people and asking for their personal information, claiming they need it in order to send the flex card, or they're asking for credit card or bank account information so you can purchase the card.

Keep in mind: You'll get a flex card automatically if you sign up for a Medicare Advantage plan that offers one, and you don't need to order one or pay extra for it. Someone won't call out of the blue to send you one.

MEDICARE IMPOSTOR SCAMS

In this scam, you may receive a call claiming to be from Medicare asking for personal information to pay your bill or settle a claim. The caller may say that your Medicare coverage will be canceled if you don't pay up quickly, and they may ask for your Medicare number, Social Security number, bank account information, credit card number, or other personal information that can help them steal your money and your identity.

This scam is similar to other government impostor scams, where criminals pretend to be from the Internal Revenue Service or Social Security Administration and make you worry that you'll lose benefits or a refund if you don't act quickly. Medicare representatives won't call you unless you have an appointment, and they won't cancel your coverage before sending several bills and a delinquency notice.

HOW TO REPORT MEDICARE SCAMS

There are several places to report Medicare scams and to get help if you find suspicious activity on your MSN.

Senior Medicare Patrol

There are volunteers in each state called Senior Medicare Patrols (SMPs) who can provide personalized assistance if you suspect Medicare fraud. They can answer questions about possible scams, help you gather evidence, and report the suspected scam to the US Department of Health and Human Services Office of Inspector General, which investigates Medicare fraud. To find SMP help in your state, you can visit the "SMP Resource Center" page on https://smpresource.org or by calling 1-877-808-2468. Their website is also a great source of information about recent Medicare-related scams.

Your local SHIP (www.shiphelp.org or 1-877-839-2675) can also be a good resource. They often work with SMP and can connect you with Medicare scam experts in your area.

Medicare Help Line

Call 1-800-MEDICARE (1-800-633-4227) to report suspected fraud or suspicious information on your MSN.

HHS Office of Inspector General

The US Department of Health and Human Services Office of Inspector General (HHS-OIG) investigates Medicare fraud. They generally won't help with your personal case, but they gather information to build a Medicare fraud case on a larger scale and impose fines and penalties on the perpetrators. You can report suspected fraud to their hotline at 1-800-447-8477 or file an online report by going to https://oig.hhs.gov and clicking on "Submit a Complaint." See the website for alerts and recent enforcement actions.

Unfortunately, there was an alert that scammers have even been spoofing HHS-OIG phone numbers and impersonating employees to steal personal information. Always remember that no government agency will call and ask for your personal information—especially your Social Security number, Medicare card number, or bank account information—over the phone.

Reporting Medicare-Related Scams in Private Health Plans

If you have a Medicare Advantage plan, Part D prescription drug coverage, or a Medigap policy, you can still get help from the Senior Medicare Patrol or by calling 1-800-MEDICARE, but also report suspected fraud on those policies to the plan. Your plan's contract should include information about where to report fraud.

TAX-DEDUCTIBLE MEDICARE COSTS

Tax Breaks Help You Save Money

Several Medicare-related expenses are tax-deductible, which can help you stretch your healthcare dollars. But you must meet certain requirements to be eligible for this break: You must itemize your income-tax deductions rather than taking the standard deduction, and you can only deduct the portion of your medical expenses that is more than 7.5% of your adjusted gross income. For example, if your adjusted gross income is $100,000 and you have $10,000 in tax-deductible medical expenses, you can only deduct $2,500 in eligible medical expenses. That said, you may be able to take a valuable deduction in years when your adjusted gross income is low and your out-of-pocket medical expenses are high. Ultimately, your eligible medical expenses can add up even if you are healthy because you can also deduct your Medicare premiums.

The following sections detail some of Medicare-related expenses that are tax-deductible.

PREMIUMS

You can deduct premiums for Medicare Part A (if you don't qualify for premium-free Part A), Part B, Part D, Medicare Advantage, and Medigap premiums. Medicare premiums can be tax-deductible even if you pay them automatically from your Social Security benefits. If you have to pay the IRMAA (the high-income surcharge for Part B and Part D), those extra premiums are also tax-deductible.

You can also deduct premiums for eligible long-term care insurance policies, with the amount based on your age.

OUT-OF-POCKET COSTS

You can deduct any out-of-pocket costs you pay yourself, including deductibles and copayments for Part A, Part B, Medicare Advantage, and Part D. These costs aren't deductible if they are covered by a Medigap, a retiree plan, or other supplemental policy.

UNCOVERED MEDICAL COSTS

If you don't have coverage for vision, dental, or hearing care, those costs can be tax-deductible. If you have insurance for some of these expenses but have to pay out-of-pocket costs after you reach a coverage cap or for copayments, the portion you pay can be tax-deductible. You can also deduct at least part of the cost for eyeglasses, contact lenses, and hearing aids if not covered in full by insurance.

Medicare has very limited coverage for acupuncture and treatments from a chiropractor, and you can deduct any portion of those costs that aren't covered.

PRESCRIPTION DRUGS

You can deduct your out-of-pocket costs, including deductibles and coinsurance or copayments. You can also deduct the cost of prescription drugs that are prescribed by your doctor but aren't covered by your Part D plan.

OTHER TAX DEDUCTIONS

You can deduct the portion of the cost of medically necessary medical equipment and supplies that isn't covered by Medicare or other insurance. Additionally, you may be able to deduct transportation expenses and lodging (up to limits) for trips primarily to receive medical care.

For a full list of eligible expenses and requirements, see IRS Publication 502, Medical and Dental Expenses, at IRS.gov.

Special Tax Breaks for the Self-Employed

If you're self-employed, you may be eligible to deduct your Medicare premiums as a business expense rather than an itemized deduction and without the 7.5% adjusted gross income threshold. You'd report the premiums on Schedule 1 of your 1040, "Self-employed health insurance deduction." Fill out IRS Form 7206 at www.irs.gov/pub/irs-pdf/f7206.pdf to calculate the deduction. The premiums can't be more than the amount you earned from the business for the year. For more information, see the Instructions to Form 1040 at IRS.gov.

TAX-FREE MEDICARE HSA EXPENSES

You can't contribute to a health savings account (HSA) after you enroll in Medicare, but if you amassed money in the account before then, you can take tax-free withdrawals for eligible medical expenses, which includes Medicare premiums after you turn sixty-five. You can withdraw money tax-free from your HSA to pay premiums for Medicare Part A, Part B, Part D, and Medicare Advantage plans but not Medigap. You can withdraw this money to reimburse yourself even if you paid Medicare premiums automatically from your Social Security benefits, and there's no time limit for withdrawing the money from the HSA for eligible premiums (or other eligible medical expenses) you incurred since you opened the HSA.

You can also withdraw money tax-free from the HSA for other eligible medical expenses, including long-term care insurance premiums with the amount based on your age, out-of-pocket expenses, the cost of care that isn't covered by insurance—such as dental, hearing, and vision care—prescription drug costs that aren't covered by insurance, and most of the same expenses that are eligible for the tax deduction. You can't take both the tax deduction and tax-free HSA withdrawals for the same expenses.

However, there are a few differences: You can't pay for Medigap premiums from an HSA, but you can pay for over-the-counter medicine and menstrual products, which aren't eligible for the tax deduction. Starting in 2026, you can withdraw up to $150 per month for direct primary care membership fees for individuals or up to $300 per month for family coverage.

See IRS Publication 969, Health Savings Accounts and Other Tax-Favored Health Plans, at IRS.gov for more information about the HSA rules.

Chapter 6

Making Medicare Work for You

After you enroll and start to use your benefits, you'll discover that Medicare offers a lot of programs to help people with special conditions or situations. It's easy to overlook some of the services that are available to you. But you may also find that Medicare can have complicated coverage rules that limit who is eligible, which providers they can use, and how often they can benefit from these services. Medicare Advantage and Part D prescription drug plans may offer additional programs with different requirements.

In this chapter, you'll learn about Medicare's special programs and strategies that can help you make the most of the coverage—whether you have chronic conditions, travel frequently, are helping an aging relative, or you have special care needs. Here's what you can do to get the most out of Medicare in your personal situation, and how you can make Medicare work for you.

MEDICARE COVERAGE WHEN TRAVELING

Different Medicare Plans, Different Restrictions

If you plan to spend your retirement traveling the world, you need to think about your health insurance. Medicare covers you throughout the United States, but it doesn't cover foreign travel emergencies except in very rare circumstances. Medicare Advantage plans may not even cover you outside of your region, except for emergencies. You may need to take extra steps to protect yourself from potentially large healthcare costs when traveling, especially if you're leaving the country. However, there are strategies and policies that can help. This entry talks about what you need to know if you're traveling with Medicare throughout the United States or abroad.

TRAVELING WITH ORIGINAL MEDICARE

If you have Original Medicare, you can use any doctor, provider, or hospital in the United States that participates in the Medicare program. Medicare defines the US as the fifty states, District of Columbia, Puerto Rico, the US Virgin Islands, Guam, American Samoa, and the Northern Mariana Islands.

But you have very limited coverage if you travel outside of the United States. Medicare will only cover expenses outside of the US in the following circumstances:

- You have a medical emergency when you're in the United States, but a foreign hospital is closer than the nearest US hospital that can treat you.
- You're traveling through Canada between Alaska and another US state, you have a medical emergency, and a Canadian hospital is closer than the nearest US hospital that can treat you.
- You live in the US, and a foreign hospital is closer than a US hospital that can treat you. This applies whether or not you have a medical emergency.

In these situations, Part A can cover inpatient hospital care, and Part B can cover ambulance and doctor services immediately before and during the covered hospital stay. However, it will not cover these expenses after your covered hospital stay ends—for example, it won't pay for you to go to a foreign doctor for a follow-up visit.

Foreign hospitals may not submit the claims to Medicare automatically, so you may have to pay the healthcare provider and then submit a claim to Medicare to be reimbursed for covered expenses.

Medicare can also cover some medical services you get on a cruise ship if the ship is in a US port or no more than six hours away from a US port.

The foreign travel situations that Medicare covers are so limited that you need to find some other coverage if you plan to travel internationally.

TRAVELING WITH MEDIGAP

If you have a private Medigap policy to supplement Original Medicare, you can use that policy anywhere in the US where you use

Medicare. Most Medigap policies also include some coverage for foreign travel emergencies.

Plans C, D, F, G, M, and N cover 80% of eligible medically necessary emergency care outside the United States after a $250 annual deductible, with a $50,000 lifetime limit. The care must begin during the first sixty days of your trip.

TRICARE FOR LIFE COVERAGE

If you're a military retiree with TRICARE for Life coverage, you'll have the same TRICARE coverage for foreign travel as you would as an active duty service member. Since Medicare doesn't cover foreign travel, your TRICARE for Life coverage will be primary coverage for medical expenses abroad. When you're in the United States, TRICARE for Life is secondary to Medicare, covering deductibles and copayments after Medicare pays its share.

Travel Insurance for Foreign Medical Care

If you don't have other coverage—or if your travel coverage is limited—it's a good idea to get travel medical insurance if you're traveling outside the US. These policies can cover emergency care outside of the US and medical evacuation to a hospital or other facility, which otherwise can cost tens of thousands of dollars. There are a wide variety of options; check whether the policy has preexisting condition exclusions or coverage limits.

TRAVELING WITH PART D

You can use most Part D plans throughout the United States. If you expect to do a lot of traveling, find out whether the plan has preferred pharmacies in the areas you're visiting. Some Part D plans have national pharmacy chains with low copayments in their preferred network.

TRAVELING WITH
MEDICARE ADVANTAGE

Even if you're just traveling in the United States, you may have limited coverage with a Medicare Advantage plan. It depends on how far the plan's network reaches. Some plans (mostly HMOs) don't cover out-of-network care except for emergencies. Other plans (PPOs) may provide some coverage out of the plan's network, but you'll usually have higher copayments and a higher out-of-network maximum. Before you travel, find out whether there are any in-network providers or facilities in the area you're visiting.

Some Medicare Advantage plans have regional or national coverage networks, and they could have in-network providers even if you're traveling to another state. If you plan to travel within the United States during the upcoming year, check the plan's provider network during open enrollment and find out whether it covers doctors and hospitals where you're going—especially if you plan to stay for a while.

Like Original Medicare, Medicare Advantage plans rarely cover care outside the United States.

MEDICARE AND CHRONIC CONDITIONS

Find Out about Special Programs

People with chronic health conditions have special coverage needs. They usually have long-standing relationships with their providers, may have high prescription drug costs, and it can be complicated to coordinate their care among several doctors and specialists.

Original Medicare and Medicare Advantage plans have recently introduced programs targeted toward people with chronic conditions. These programs provide specialized coverage and care navigation that people often overlook, whether you have a condition such as diabetes, kidney failure, heart disease, cancer, respiratory disease, or other long-term conditions.

CHRONIC CONDITIONS AND ORIGINAL MEDICARE

There are some benefits to choosing Original Medicare if you have chronic conditions—especially the ability to use any provider who participates in the program. People with chronic conditions often have strong ties to their providers and practices and may not want to run the risk of losing coverage if their provider leaves a Medicare Advantage network.

You don't need a referral to see a specialist, and you can get most services without prior authorization restrictions. If you have Original Medicare with a Medigap policy, you'll have to pay regular premiums, but you won't have larger out-of-pocket costs even if you have a lot of healthcare needs. You may need to see a doctor more frequently than people without chronic conditions, and you may even need some care while you're on vacation, which is another benefit to being able to use Medicare throughout the country.

As mentioned before, Original Medicare has introduced some special programs to help people with chronic conditions navigate their care. See the following program descriptions to learn a little more.

Chronic Care Management Services

If you have two or more serious chronic conditions that you expect to last at least a year, Medicare Part B can pay for a healthcare provider to help to manage your care for those conditions. Your provider creates a comprehensive care plan, reviews your medicine, and can meet with you on a monthly basis. You pay the annual Part B deductible and 20% coinsurance, like you would with other doctors' visits.

Principal Illness Navigation Services

If you have a serious condition that is expected to last at least three months and puts you at risk for hospitalization and other issues, Part B covers monthly navigation services to help you understand your condition or diagnosis and guide you through the healthcare system. The services can last for up to a year. Coverage is also subject to the Part B deductible and 20% coinsurance.

Part D and Chronic Conditions

If you have a chronic condition, it's essential to check how the Part D plan covers your drugs. The $2,000 out-of-pocket spending cap that took effect in 2025 (which rose to $2,100 in 2026) is especially helpful for people with chronic conditions and high drug costs. Make sure your drugs are included in the plan's formulary during open enrollment each year; otherwise, they aren't protected by the cap. If you have high front-end drug costs, consider signing up for the Medicare Prescription Payment Plan, the smoothing program that spreads your out-of-pocket drug costs over the year.

MEDICARE ADVANTAGE AND CHRONIC CONDITIONS

Medicare Advantage has several special programs for people with chronic conditions. But first, make sure your providers and facilities are covered. Some academic medical centers aren't covered by Medicare Advantage plans, which could limit your access to some programs focusing on your condition. Also, find out about coverage for your special needs if you plan to do any traveling; an example would be finding in-network dialysis centers outside of your area.

Special Benefits for People with Chronic Conditions

Medicare Advantage plans have been able to offer special health benefits to people with chronic conditions since 2019, including coverage for transportation to medical appointments, over-the-counter medicine, and nutrition counseling. Starting in 2020, the plans could add special nonmedical benefits for people with chronic conditions—called Special Supplemental Benefits for the Chronically Ill (SSBCI)—such as a grocery allowance, transportation to nonmedical needs.

Not all plans offer these benefits, and eligibility is limited to people with certain chronic conditions. Before choosing a plan during open enrollment, find out about the details of the coverage and eligibility, and put it into perspective—transportation benefits can be helpful, but it's even more important to make sure your doctors and facilities are covered.

Chronic Condition Special Needs Plans

Medicare Advantage special needs plans (SNPs) were introduced in 2006, and they've become much more popular over the past few years. In 2025, 21% of Medicare Advantage enrollees are in SNPs, up from 14% in 2020, according to research organization KFF. These plans provide specialized coverage for people in three situations: people who have both Medicare and Medicaid (called dual eligible special needs plans, or D-SNPs); people with chronic conditions (C-SNPs); and people who live in an institutional setting such as a nursing home (I-SNPs). In 2025, 16% of the people who have SNPs are in plans focusing on chronic conditions, up from 10% in 2024.

C-SNPs offer specialized coverage for people with chronic conditions such as diabetes, cardiovascular disease, respiratory disease, end-stage renal disease, and heart disease. They usually have provider networks focusing on specialists for your condition and may charge lower copayments for drugs people with your condition take. These plans also provide education to help you care for your condition, and care navigation services, where a nurse or other provider meets with you regularly to help you manage your care among several doctors and specialists. They're more likely to provide the extra benefits—such as transportation and bathroom safety devices—than regular Medicare Advantage plans. For example, a kidney care C-SNP may cover transportation to and from dialysis appointments and a grocery allowance for foods tailored to your chronic condition.

Even though the number of C-SNPs are growing, you may not have one for your condition in your area. You can search for plans in your zip code using the Medicare Plan Finder to check for SNP availability in your area.

DIABETES AND MEDICARE

Preventive Programs, Medications, and Special Coverage

Diabetes is especially prevalent in older adults. More than 24% of people age sixty-five and older in the United States have been diagnosed with diabetes, and almost 5% more have diabetes but haven't been diagnosed, according to the Centers for Disease Control and Prevention. Because of these demographics, Medicare offers programs to screen for diabetes and help prevent or delay type 2 diabetes; the system also offers special benefits for people who have been diagnosed or have other risk factors.

DIABETES PREVENTION PROGRAMS

Medicare covers several free programs that screen for diabetes and promote healthy habits to help prevent diabetes.

- **Screening:** Medicare covers up to two diabetes screenings per year if your doctor determines you're at risk for developing diabetes—such as people with high blood pressure, high blood sugar, abnormal cholesterol levels, or obesity. The screenings are free from any cost sharing.
- **Medicare Diabetes Prevention Program:** The Medicare Diabetes Prevention Program includes sixteen weekly group sessions over a six-month period focusing on changing your diet, establishing exercise routines, and controlling your weight. You can also get six

monthly follow-up sessions to help maintain the healthy habits. To qualify for the program, you must have certain glucose levels and a BMI of 25 or more (or a BMI of 23 or more if you're Asian). The program, which can be virtual or in person, must be offered by an approved supplier and is not subject to the Part B deductible or coinsurance. You can find an approved supplier in your area by using the diabetes prevention program search tool here: www.medicare.gov/coverage/medicare-diabetes-prevention-program.

- **Nutrition counseling:** Medicare offers up to three hours of medical nutrition therapy services in the first calendar year with a dietitian or other nutrition professional, and help managing lifestyle factors that affect your diabetes. You may qualify for additional hours if your doctor determines you need additional services.

In addition to these resources for prevention, there are additional tools in place for those already dealing with diabetes.

MANAGING DIABETES

Medicare offers programs to help people manage their diabetes. Some of the following options are offered depending on your plan.

- **Diabetes self-management training:** Up to one hour of individual training and nine hours of group training to help people with diabetes monitor their blood sugar, control their diet, and reduce their risks. This program is subject to the Part B deductible and 20% coinsurance.
- **Diabetes supplies:** Medicare covers blood sugar testing monitors, glucose test strips, continuous glucose monitors, and other

diabetes supplies and equipment. These supplies are covered by Part B as durable medical equipment and subject to the deductible and 20% coinsurance.

As part of managing diabetes, you also need access to proper medication. See the following section to find out more about what is covered.

MEDICINE FOR DIABETES

Medicare Part D plans must cap out-of-pocket costs for covered insulin at $35 per month, but these rules only cover the types of insulin covered on your plan's formulary. Make sure the insulin you take is covered by the plan you choose during open enrollment.

Part B covers an insulin pump that is not disposable, and the insulin used in it. Insulin covered by Part B is still subject to the $35 cap.

Part D can also cover Ozempic and other drugs that are FDA-approved for people with diabetes. Since Medicare is prohibited from covering drugs specifically used for weight loss, your doctor will have to submit prior authorization forms explaining that you have diabetes.

Special Coverages for Diabetes

Medicare will cover some services for people with diabetes that it won't cover for others. Medicare doesn't usually cover eye exams, but it will cover eye exams for people with diabetes and other risk factors to test for glaucoma and diabetic retinopathy. It doesn't cover podiatry, but it will cover foot exams every six months if you have diabetic peripheral neuropathy and therapeutic shoes and inserts.

MEDICARE ADVANTAGE
AND DIABETES

If you have a Medicare Advantage plan, make sure your specialists—especially your endocrinologist—are covered when you choose a plan each year during open enrollment. You may be eligible for special coverages for people with chronic conditions, such as transportation to doctors' appointments, a grocery allowance for healthy food, and coverage for over-the-counter benefits. Not everyone with chronic conditions qualifies for these benefits—find out whether you are eligible and how that coverage aligns with the rest of the coverage, especially the provider network and prescription drugs you take.

Chronic Condition Special Needs Plans (C-SNPs)

These Medicare Advantage plans focus on special coverage for certain chronic conditions. Some plans specialize in diabetes, which may provide a strong provider network of diabetes-related specialists, a care coordinator to help you navigate the health system, special coverage for diabetes supplies and equipment, nutrition counseling, a grocery benefit for healthy food, and drug coverage with lower copayments for diabetes medicine. The most popular type of C-SNP focuses on cardiovascular disorders and/or diabetes, according to a study by benefits consulting firm Milliman. In 2024, there were 205 of those plans throughout the country.

Still, diabetes-related C-SNPs aren't available in every area. You can search for them using the Medicare.gov Plan Finder and filtering for special needs plans, and you can get more information by contacting the plan. Don't forget to ask your endocrinologist's office about plans they participate in.

PAIN MANAGEMENT PROGRAMS AND MEDICARE

Expanded Coverage for Pain Relief

As problems with opioid use addiction grows among older adults, Medicare has expanded its coverage of other ways to get relief from chronic pain. In the past, Medicare did not cover chiropractors or acupuncture and had limited coverage for physical and occupational therapy. Now, Medicare will cover these forms of treatment as an alternative to opioids to help people manage their pain. However, the coverage is limited to very specific situations. Here's when you can get coverage for these services.

CHIROPRACTIC SERVICES

Medicare Part B covers chiropractic services in one situation: The manual manipulation of the spine when it's medically necessary to correct subluxation, which is the misalignment of the spine—defined by Medicare as when the spinal joints fail to move properly, but the contact between the joints remains intact. Medicare will cover the realignment of the spine and chronic subluxation as long as the patient is improving, but it won't cover maintenance care after the spine has been realigned. It covers X-rays ordered by a doctor to show that the spinal subluxation needs treatment, but not X-rays ordered by a chiropractor.

These services are subject to the Part B deductible and 20% coinsurance. Medicare Advantage plans may have different copayments. Some also cover routine chiropractic visits as an additional benefit.

ACUPUNCTURE

Medicare didn't cover acupuncture at all until 2020, but now it covers it in one situation: Medicare Part B covers acupuncture (including dry needling) to treat chronic lower back pain. If you've had low back pain for at least twelve weeks and the pain isn't associated with another cause, such as cancer that has spread or an inflammation, you can get twelve acupuncture sessions within a ninety-day period. If your pain decreases because of the acupuncture, Medicare may pay for up to eight additional sessions. If you aren't showing improvement, however, Medicare will not cover the additional treatment. The maximum is twenty sessions a year.

Medicare also limits who it will cover to do the acupuncture, which can make it more difficult to find an eligible provider: The acupuncture must be administered by a doctor or other healthcare provider, such as a nurse practitioner or physician's assistant, who has a master's or doctoral degree in acupuncture or Oriental medicine from a school that is accredited from the Accreditation Commission for Acupuncture and Herbal Medicine. They must also have an active, unrestricted license to practice acupuncture in the state or territory where you're receiving care.

Acupuncture is subject to the Part B deductible and 20% coinsurance. Medicare Advantage plans may have different copayments, and some plans expand coverage for acupuncture beyond the lower back.

PHYSICAL THERAPY AND OCCUPATIONAL THERAPY

Medicare covers physical therapy when your doctor or other healthcare provider certifies that you need it. Outpatient physical therapy is covered by Medicare Part B and is subject to the deductible and 20% coinsurance.

You can receive outpatient physical therapy covered by Part B in a doctor's or therapist's office, an outpatient hospital department, or an outpatient rehabilitation facility. Physical therapy is also covered by Part B if you're in a skilled nursing facility or are receiving home care but don't qualify for a Part A–covered stay. Medicare also covers occupational therapy, which helps you with the activities of daily living—such as bathing, dressing, and eating—and speech-language pathology services.

In the past, there was a cap to the number of therapy services you could receive each year, but that cap was removed in 2018. Now, if your annual therapy costs reach a certain level—$2,410 for physical therapy and speech-language pathology combined in 2025, and $2,410 for occupational therapy—your provider must confirm that the therapy is medically necessary.

Medicare Part A covers physical therapy, occupational therapy, and speech-language pathology services when you are an inpatient at a hospital or a skilled nursing facility, or if you are receiving home care that is covered by Part A.

OTHER PAIN MANAGEMENT PROGRAMS

Medicare also covers other pain management programs and services, including a monthly service to help people living with chronic pain with medication management, care coordination, and planning. It also covers opioid use disorder treatment services by a doctor or other healthcare provider, which can include care management, individual and group therapy, and substance use counseling.

Tax-Free HSA Withdrawals for Pain Management

Even though Medicare only covers these pain management programs in limited situations, eligible withdrawals from HSAs are much broader. If you already have money in an HSA, you can withdraw it tax-free to pay for a chiropractor, acupuncturist, and physical therapist without Medicare's restrictions on the type of service they provide. Even though you can't contribute to an HSA after you enroll in Medicare, you can withdraw money from the account tax-free for eligible expenses any time in the future.

DEMENTIA AND ALZHEIMER'S COVERAGE

Financial Help with Screening, Drugs, and Special Programs

A large number of older adults suffer from memory loss as they get older, which can develop into debilitating dementia and Alzheimer's disease. A 2024 study of Medicare data by researchers at the Milken Institute School of Public Health (George Washington University) and NORC at the University of Chicago found that about 9% of all Medicare beneficiaries may have Alzheimer's disease or related dementia.

Medicare covers many dementia-related expenses, and coverage is evolving to keep up with new developments in screenings and medications. However, Medicare leaves out one of the biggest expenses for many people with dementia: The cost of long-term care in a nursing home, assisted living facility, or a memory care unit. This entry details what Medicare does cover and how the rules have been changing.

DEMENTIA SCREENING

It can be difficult to screen for Alzheimer's and dementia, but Medicare covers some tests that can help. The annual Medicare wellness visit covers a cognitive assessment without being subject to the deductible or coinsurance. If the doctor discovers anything,

Medicare Part B can also cover a separate visit to review your cognitive function. That visit is subject to the Part B deductible and 20% coinsurance.

Part B can also cover diagnostic testing for Alzheimer's. A PET scan can show if there are beta-amyloid plaques or tau tangles (misshapen proteins that are indicators of Alzheimer's) in the brain. Medicare expanded the coverage for the PET scans in October 2023, no longer limiting the coverage to one amyloid PET scan during your lifetime. This change is helpful because Medicare requires patients to have amyloid plaques before covering Alzheimer's medications such as Leqembi.

CARE PLANNING AND COORDINATION

Medicare covers care planning and coordination for people with cognitive impairment. This provides Medicare beneficiaries with information about medical and nonmedical treatment, clinical trials, and support services available in the community.

ALZHEIMER'S AND DEMENTIA DRUGS

Medicare Part D covers several drugs for people with dementia, including at least two cholinesterase inhibitors. Check the plan's formulary at www.medicare.gov/plan-compare to find out whether the Part D plan you're considering covers the medications. These drugs may have prior authorization requirements.

Medicare Part B covers drugs that are given intravenously by a doctor or other healthcare provider. This includes Alzheimer's treatments that have full FDA approval but not those that have gone through accelerated FDA approval. It can cover Leqembi (lecanemab), which was granted traditional approval by the FDA in 2023, and Kisunla (donanemab), which received FDA approval in 2024, in certain situations: You must be diagnosed with mild cognitive impairment and have documented evidence of beta-amyloid plaques on the brain, and use a doctor who participates in a qualifying registry. The drugs are not approved for treating advanced stages of Alzheimer's.

MEDICARE AND MEMORY CARE

Medicare doesn't cover custodial care, which is the help with activities of daily living (such as bathing, eating, dressing, and transferring) in a nursing home, assisted living facility, your own home, or a memory care unit. Medicare provides limited coverage for home care if a doctor certifies that you are homebound and need intermittent skilled nursing—but not if you only need custodial care.

Medicare Advantage and Dementia

Medicare Advantage plans must provide at least as much coverage as Original Medicare, but they may have more prior authorization requirements, and they do have provider networks. Make sure your neurologist is covered. You can compare medical and drug costs and coverage for plans in your area during open enrollment at www.medicare.gov/plan-compare.

HELP FOR DEMENTIA FAMILY CAREGIVERS

The Guiding an Improved Dementia Experience (GUIDE) Model is a program that provides support for people with dementia and their unpaid caregivers. The program was launched in 2024, and over three hundred organizations are currently participating in the model.

The program is designed to coordinate care for patients with dementia and help their unpaid caregivers. It includes an assessment with a doctor or care team to create a care plan. It also provides caregiver training and access to a care navigator who helps people with dementia and their caregivers access services and supports. Additionally, the program offers a stipend to help pay for respite services at home or in an adult day care center to give caregivers a break. Medicare pays participating organizations each month to provide these services. The patients usually don't have out-of-pocket costs for these services.

To qualify, the patient must be enrolled in Original Medicare; it is not available to people in Medicare Advantage programs. They must have a dementia diagnosis, not just mild cognitive impairment. They cannot be in hospice or a resident of a nursing home.

For more information, see CMS's GUIDE Model Overview factsheet (www.cms.gov/files/document/guide-model-overview-fs .pdf) or contact one of the participating programs (for details and a map with participating programs, visit: www.cms.gov/priorities/ innovation/where-innovation-happening#model=guiding-an-improved-dementia-experience-guide-model).

HELP WITH MEDICARE AND DEMENTIA COVERAGE

For help learning about what Medicare covers for dementia or Alzheimer's, contact your local SHIP. You can also get more information from the Alzheimer's Association. Your neurologist's office can also help you and your caregivers understand what is and is not covered by Medicare, requirements before the program will cover certain tests or medications, and other resources that can help.

MENTAL HEALTH COVERAGE

An Expanded Network with More Providers

Medicare's coverage of mental health has improved significantly over the past several years. In the past, Medicare beneficiaries had to pay a higher percentage of the cost of outpatient mental health services than they did for other doctors' services. But after recognizing the growing need for mental health services for older adults, Medicare expanded the amount of coverage to be closer to its payments for other healthcare services. Medicare also expanded the types of mental health services and providers it covers in 2024 to make mental healthcare more accessible to people with Medicare.

INPATIENT MENTAL HEALTH COVERAGE

If you're admitted to a general or psychiatric hospital as an inpatient, you pay the same cost sharing as you do for other inpatient hospital stays: Part A hospital deductible (which is $1,676 in 2025), no coinsurance for days one through sixty, and daily coinsurance for days sixty-one to ninety (which is $419 in 2025).

However, there is one big difference: Medicare will only cover 190 days in your *lifetime* for a hospital that specializes in mental health. But days spent in a general hospital, even for mental health conditions, don't count toward the 190-day limit.

OUTPATIENT MENTAL HEALTH COVERAGE

Medicare Part B covers outpatient mental health services in a doctor's or therapist's office, a community health center, or other outpatient facility. It covers care from psychiatrists, clinical psychologists, clinical social workers, clinical nurse specialists, nurse practitioners, and physician assistants. Starting in 2024, licensed marriage and family therapists and mental health counselors, including addiction counselors, can also choose to enroll in Medicare and be covered by the program.

Until recently, Medicare beneficiaries had to pay a higher percentage of the cost for outpatient mental health services than they did for other doctors' services—paying 50% of the cost rather than 20% for other doctors' services. But the rules changed in 2008 and were phased in over the next few years. Now, Medicare pays 80% of the Medicare-approved amount, and you pay the standard Part B 20% coinsurance for mental health services just like you do for other doctors' services.

Additionally, Medicare expanded some mental health coverage in 2024: Medicare Part B now pays for partial hospitalization programs for people who need at least twenty hours of treatment per week, but don't stay in a facility overnight. The doctor must certify that you would otherwise need inpatient treatment. Part B can now also cover intensive outpatient services for people who need nine to twenty hours per week. The need must be confirmed by a physician every other month.

FINDING A MENTAL
HEALTH PROVIDER

Sometimes it can be difficult to find a mental health provider who accepts Medicare, especially one that is accepting new patients. Even though only about 1% of physicians who aren't pediatricians have opted out of the Medicare program, 8.1% of psychiatrists opted out in 2024, according to KFF. Psychiatrists accounted for the 39% of the physicians who opted out of Medicare in 2024. These psychiatrists accept cash rather than Medicare. And even psychiatrists who haven't opted out aren't necessarily accepting new patients. Finding a mental health provider can be especially difficult in rural areas.

To find a psychiatrist in your area who accepts Medicare, use the Medicare Care Compare tool at www.medicare.gov/care-compare. The tool also lets you know whether the physician accepts assignment or if they charge up to 15% more than the Medicare-approved amount.

SPECIAL TELEHEALTH RULES
FOR BEHAVIORAL HEALTH

If you have difficulty finding a mental health provider who accepts Medicare in your area, you may have more success finding care through telehealth. Coverage for telehealth services were expanded during COVID-19, but coverage for many of those services ended on September 30, 2025. However, Medicare created special telehealth rules for behavioral health services—continuing to cover telehealth for mental health counselors, marriage and family therapists, and other mental health providers after that date. Telehealth is covered under Part B with 20% coinsurance, just like other doctors' services.

MEDICARE AND MENTAL HEALTH SCREENING

Medicare also covers some mental health–related screenings with no cost sharing, including:

- One depression screening each year as a Part B preventive service without a deductible or coinsurance, if you go to a primary care provider who accepts the Medicare-approved amount.
- The "Welcome to Medicare" preventive visit includes a review of possible risk factors for depression.
- Discussion of mental health status during the annual wellness visit.
- One alcohol misuse screening per year, and four counseling sessions per year.
- Up to eight tobacco cessation counseling sessions in a twelve-month period.

MEDICARE ADVANTAGE AND MENTAL HEALTH

Medicare Advantage plans must cover at least as much as Original Medicare, but the cost sharing can be different.

A large portion of Medicare Advantage plans require prior authorization for some mental health coverage in 2025, including inpatient stays in a psychiatric hospital (93%), partial hospitalization (88%), opioid treatment program services (83%), mental health specialty services (80%), psychiatric services (80%), and outpatient substance abuse services (78%), according to KFF.

If you plan to use a psychiatrist, find out which psychiatrists in your area are included in the Medicare Advantage plan's network before choosing a plan—some Medicare Advantage plans do not have many psychiatrists available in certain counties.

Part D Prescription Drug Coverage and Mental Health

Mental health medications are generally covered by Part D. All Part D plans must cover antidepressant, anticonvulsant, and antipsychotic medications. Part D plans can also cover other prescription drugs for mental health on their formularies; the plan may require prior authorization first. The costs can vary by plan. Use the Medicare Plan Finder to find out how each plan in your area covers your drugs.

MEDICARE AND WEIGHT LOSS DRUGS AND PROGRAMS

More Coverage but Still Some Gaps

Obesity is a growing health issue for older adults, and it can lead to other expensive health problems, including cardiovascular disease, diabetes, depression, and disability. Obesity is defined as a BMI of more than 30 (BMI is the relationship of height to weight). In 2021–2023, 38.9% of adults age sixty and older were considered to be obese, according to the National Center for Health Statistics.

Medicare has been investing in programs and procedures to help with obesity, but so far it hasn't covered weight loss drugs. The 2003 Medicare Modernization Act that created Medicare Part D prohibited Medicare plans from covering drugs prescribed specifically for weight loss, in part because there were safety concerns about some of the weight loss drugs on the market at the time.

That said, the weight loss drug landscape changed with the development of glucagon-like peptide-1 (GLP-1) agonists. These drugs were created to treat type 2 diabetes, but they have also been found to help with weight loss. Novo Nordisk's Ozempic, which has been approved by the FDA for diabetes, can also help with weight loss. The company subsequently introduced Wegovy, another version of the drug with the same underlying product, semaglutide. That drug was approved by the FDA for weight loss for people with a BMI of 30 or higher, or with a BMI of 27 or higher and at least one weight-related issue, such as high blood pressure or high cholesterol. But neither drug can currently be covered by Medicare when prescribed specifically for weight loss.

The Trump administration proposed a five-year demonstration project that would begin in 2027 for Medicare and allow Medicare Part D plans to cover GLP-1 agonists to treat obesity in certain areas of the country. Details have not yet been finalized.

WEIGHT LOSS DRUGS FOR OTHER CONDITIONS

Even though many people use GLP-1 agonists like Ozempic and Wegovy to lose weight, Medicare won't cover it specifically for that purpose. This is a big surprise to people who had coverage for weight loss drugs when they had employer insurance while working and planned to continue taking the medication for the long term, but then lost coverage for it when they retired and enrolled in Medicare. These medications can cost more than $1,000 per month without insurance.

Most Medicare Part D plans do cover Ozempic for people with diabetes, but not for weight loss. Your doctor usually needs to complete prior authorization requirements and provide evidence that you have diabetes before you can get the medication covered.

In March 2024, the FDA approved Wegovy for people who have cardiovascular disease and are also overweight. Now, eligible people with cardiovascular disease can get coverage for Wegovy if their Medicare Part D plan offers it. They will generally need to complete prior authorization requirements showing that they have cardiovascular disease and meet other qualifications.

Eli Lilly's Mounjaro (tirzepatide) and Zepbound have been used for weight loss too. Mounjaro is FDA-approved for diabetes. Zepbound is FDA-approved for weight loss, and in December 2024 the

FDA approved it to treat moderate to severe sleep apnea for adults with obesity.

Even though Part D plans are allowed to cover Wegovy for eligible people with heart disease, many plans still do not cover it. When comparing plans during open enrollment each year it's essential to find out whether the drug is covered on the plan's formulary. You can go to the Medicare Plan Finder at Medicare.gov and type in your drug and dosages, and then sort plans by lowest drug and premium cost to quickly find which ones cover the medication. Also, remember that even if the drug is on a plan's formulary, that doesn't mean you're automatically covered—your doctor will generally need to complete prior authorization requirements first.

If you're seeing a doctor for weight loss, talk to them about Medicare coverage for the drugs you take and any alternatives that may be covered. They usually have experience navigating the insurance coverage issues for these medications.

MEDICARE COVERAGE FOR WEIGHT LOSS COUNSELING

If you have a BMI of 30 or higher, Medicare Part B can cover weight loss counseling as a free preventive benefit without being subject to the deductible or coinsurance. Your primary care provider does the counseling and creates a personalized prevention plan to coordinate with your other care.

Part B also covers medical nutritional services for people who have diabetes or kidney disease, or who had a kidney transplant in the past thirty-six months. A doctor must refer you for the services, which must be provided by a registered dietitian or other nutrition professional who meets certain requirements.

Medicare Advantage Plans with Extra Weight Loss Benefits

Private Medicare Advantage plans must provide at least as much coverage as Original Medicare, and they may also provide some extra coverage to help people with weight loss, such as gym memberships and a grocery allowance for healthy food. But before choosing a plan for these extra perks, make sure your drugs and doctors are covered. Remember that Medicare Advantage plans must follow the same Part D rules for prescription drugs and currently are not allowed to cover drugs prescribed specifically for weight loss.

MEDICARE AND WEIGHT LOSS SURGERY

Medicare covers some types of bariatric surgery procedures—such as gastric bypass surgery and laparoscopic gastric banding surgery—for people with a BMI of 35 or higher and other conditions, such as diabetes or heart disease. You also need to show that obesity treatment or counseling hasn't worked in the past. Medicare will not cover surgery considered to be cosmetic, such as liposuction.

MEDICARE AND PREVENTIVE CARE

Special Programs to Keep You Healthy

Medicare has been investing more money into preventive care to try to catch diseases early and reduce care costs. The Affordable Care Act reduced or eliminated a lot of preventive care's deductibles and copayments, and the Inflation Reduction Act expanded the preventive care provisions.

In addition to vaccines and screenings for diseases, Medicare also offers several preventive care counseling and education programs to help prevent certain conditions from becoming more severe. This entry provides more information on several preventive care programs that are covered by Medicare and who is eligible to benefit. These programs are covered under Part B and generally are not subject to the deductible or the 20% coinsurance.

MEDICARE DIABETES PREVENTION PROGRAM

People with prediabetes have high blood sugar levels, but they're not high enough to be diagnosed with type 2 diabetes. Taking steps to improve your diet and exercise at that point can help prevent the progression to type 2 diabetes. To find more information about how this Medicare Diabetes Prevention Program might work for you, refer to the Diabetes and Medicare entry earlier in this chapter.

DIABETES
SELF-MANAGEMENT TRAINING

If you've been diagnosed with diabetes, Medicare Part B can cover diabetes self-management training to help you manage the disease. To find more information about how this program might work for you, refer to the Diabetes and Medicare entry earlier in this chapter.

MEDICAL NUTRITION THERAPY

Medicare Part B covers nutrition therapy services for people with diabetes or kidney disease or who have had a kidney transplant in the past thirty-six months. A doctor must refer you for the services. You can get three hours of medical nutrition therapy services in the first calendar year, and your doctor can give you a referral for more hours—with up to two hours of follow-up services each year. The services must be provided by a registered dietitian or nutritional professional who meets certain requirements.

OBESITY BEHAVIORAL THERAPY

Medicare Part B covers obesity screenings and behavioral counseling for people with a BMI of 30 or more. This program includes a dietary assessment and counseling to help you lose weight through diet and exercise. Your primary care doctor or other primary care provider gives the counseling in a primary care setting (such as a doctor's office) and creates a personalized prevention plan to coordinate with the rest of your care.

ALCOHOL MISUSE SCREENINGS AND COUNSELING

Medicare Part B covers one alcohol misuse screening each year for adults who use alcohol but aren't considered alcohol dependent. If your primary care provider or other healthcare provider determines you are misusing alcohol, you can get up to four face-to-face counseling sessions each year. You must get the counseling in a primary care setting.

SEXUALLY TRANSMITTED INFECTION SCREENINGS AND COUNSELING

Medicare Part B covers screenings for sexually transmitted infections, including chlamydia, gonorrhea, syphilis, and hepatitis B if you're pregnant or are at increased risk for a sexually transmitted infection. Medicare also covers up to two face-to-face behavioral counseling sessions of twenty to thirty minutes if you're at increased risk for these infections. Medicare covers sexually transmitted infection screenings once every twelve months, and up to two behavioral counseling sessions each year. Your healthcare provider must order the screening or refer you to the counseling, which must be in a primary care setting.

COUNSELING TO PREVENT TOBACCO-CAUSED DISEASES

Medicare Part B covers counseling to help you stop smoking or using tobacco. You can get up to eight counseling sessions in a twelve-month period.

Find Out If You're Eligible for Preventive Programs

Medicare Part B offers a variety of programs to help detect disease and prevent it from progressing, including vaccines, screenings, and counseling programs. Most are not subject to the Part B deductible or the 20% coinsurance. You can get a list of the preventive programs available at www.medicare.gov/coverage/preventive-screening-services.

MEDICARE AND HOSPICE CARE

Special Coverage for End-of-Life Care

Hospice care provides comfort care rather than medical treatment to cure your illness at the end of your life. A hospice team can manage your care when you are expected to live no more than six months. The team focuses on taking steps to help you live as comfortably as possible during that time and providing emotional, social, and spiritual support. People who receive hospice care have chronic conditions that can no longer be treatable, such as Alzheimer's disease, dementia, heart disease, Parkinson's disease, or other conditions.

Medicare Part A covers hospice care at your home, an inpatient hospice center, or within a nursing home or other facility. The care must be provided by a Medicare-approved hospice provider. Your doctor can help you find an approved hospice provider, or you can find one in your area by going to www.medicare.gov/care-compare.

WHO IS ELIGIBLE FOR HOSPICE CARE?

To receive hospice care, your doctor or a hospice doctor must certify that you are terminally ill and have a life expectancy of six months or less. You must sign a statement choosing to receive hospice care (palliative care) rather than other treatments to cure your illness. You and your family will work with the hospice provider to set up a care plan.

You can get hospice care for up to two ninety-day periods, followed by an unlimited number of sixty-day periods. At the start of the first ninety-day benefit period, your doctor or your hospice doctor must certify that you have a life expectancy of less than six months. After that first ninety-day benefit period, the hospice medical director or hospice doctor must recertify that you're terminally ill with a life expectancy of less than six months. There is not a six-month limit on hospice care, however—you can continue to receive hospice care beyond that time if your doctor certifies that you have a life expectancy of no more than six months at the time. You can continue to receive treatment for unrelated conditions.

If your health improves, you may not want to continue to receive hospice care. You can change your mind and discontinue hospice at any time if you decide to receive treatment for your condition instead. You will have to sign a form specifying the date your hospice care will end.

COVERED HOSPICE SERVICES

Medicare covers most of your medical expenses if you are on hospice care. Your hospice team creates a care plan that can include services from a doctor and nursing care, drugs to help control your pain, health aide services, medical equipment and supplies, social worker services, and other services to manage your terminal illness and related conditions. Hospice can also provide grief and loss counseling for you and your family.

Medicare also covers respite care if your usual caregiver, such as a family member, needs rest from caregiving. You can get inpatient respite care in a Medicare-approved hospice inpatient facility, such as a hospital or nursing home. You can stay up to five days each time you need respite care. You can get respite care more than once, but only on an occasional basis.

COSTS OF HOSPICE CARE

If you sign up for hospice care, you have very few out-of-pocket costs. You continue to pay your Part B premiums (and Part A premiums if you don't qualify for premium-free coverage). But you don't pay regular Medicare deductibles and copayments. Instead, you may have two key expenses:

1. Up to a $5 copay for prescription drugs used to control the symptoms and pain from your terminal illness.
2. Up to 5% of the cost of inpatient respite care, if you have a short-term inpatient stay in a Medicare-approved hospice facility, hospital, or skilled nursing facility to give your caregiver a break.

You may still have to pay room and board if you live in a nursing home or other facility and you choose to get hospice care. Note that if you have a Medigap plan, it will cover your copayments for hospice drugs and respite care. All Medigap plans cover the hospice care coinsurance or copayment in full or in part.

Hospice Care for Medicare Advantage

Original Medicare will cover your hospice benefits, even if you're in a Medicare Advantage plan. If you have Medicare Advantage, you can keep it and pay premiums if you want coverage for care that isn't related to hospice. Your Medicare Advantage plan must help you find a Medicare-approved hospice provider in your area.

WHERE TO GET HELP WITH HOSPICE CARE

You can find out more about the hospice providers in your area from your State Health Insurance Assistance Program. Your doctor can also let you or your caregivers know about hospice facilities and when you may be ready. The Hospice Foundation of America is a nonprofit organization that provides information and programs about hospice care for families and professionals.

CAREGIVERS AND MEDICARE

What to Know When Helping Aging Relatives

Adult children who are younger than sixty-five often end up getting a crash course in Medicare as their parents age and need help making medical and financial decisions. Sometimes these children are thrown into this role quickly if their loved one ends up in the hospital after a fall or medical event. This entry offers some key information for caregivers to know about Medicare coverage.

REVIEW THE "MEDICARE & YOU" HANDBOOK

This is the best resource about Medicare and the decisions you can help your aging relatives make each year. The booklet also includes information about what's covered, what you need to do during open enrollment, how to review and appeal claims, where to get help, and other information. Medicare beneficiaries receive it in the mail each year, but you can access it any time from their online Medicare account or at Medicare.gov.

GET PERMISSION TO TALK WITH MEDICARE

You'll need permission to talk with Medicare about your parents' medical and billing issues. Fill out the Authorization to Disclose Personal Health Information release form at Medicare.gov.

Get Healthcare Power of Attorney Documents

The Medicare authorization form gives you permission to talk with Medicare on someone else's behalf, but you'll need a healthcare power of attorney (also called a healthcare proxy) to be able to make medical decisions for them if they're unable to do so themselves. You can get this legal document at the same time as a financial power of attorney so you will have permission to help with their financial affairs too.

REVIEW THEIR ANNUAL NOTICE OF CHANGE

Medicare beneficiaries who have a Part D or Medicare Advantage plan receive an Annual Notice of Change document in September each year, outlining changes to their Part D or Medicare Advantage plan's coverage and costs for the upcoming year. Even if their current policy has been working well, it's important to review this document and make sure the plan still provides the coverage they need. Plans can change their costs, coverage, lists of covered drugs, and, for Medicare Advantage plans, their provider networks. If you don't do anything, their current coverage will generally continue, but don't assume that everything that worked for the plan in the past will remain the same the following year.

HELP WITH OPEN ENROLLMENT DECISIONS

Medicare beneficiaries need to make some key decisions about Medicare during open enrollment every year, which runs from October 15 to December 7 for new coverage starting January 1. If they have Original Medicare, they may have a separate Part D plan to cover prescription drugs. They (potentially with your help) need to review the Part D policies available in their area each year and choose the one with the best combination of costs and coverage for their prescriptions. It's essential to make sure that the drugs they take are covered by the plan's formulary. If they have a Medicare Advantage plan, that plan can provide both medical and drug coverage. Check coverage for the drugs they use and make sure the doctors and hospitals they prefer are included in the plan's network. You can compare options at www.medicare.gov/plan-compare.

REVIEW THEIR MEDICARE SUMMARY NOTICES (MSN)

This document is similar to an Explanation of Benefits (EOB) from a private insurer; it shows the claims that were paid, which providers or hospitals they used, any portion that wasn't covered, and how to appeal a denial. They'll receive a paper document every four months listing their claims, with separate documents for Part A, Part B, and durable medical equipment. You can also access this information faster by signing up for an online Medicare account. Look for errors, unexpected charges, and suspicious activity, which could be a clue about Medicare fraud. If they have Part D prescription drug coverage, they'll receive a separate EOB. If they have a Medicare Advantage plan, they'll receive that EOB instead.

GET ACCESS TO THEIR ONLINE MEDICARE ACCOUNT

Signing up for an online Medicare account is a great way to get information about their coverage and claims, and you can keep track of their prescriptions and preventive care options there too. You can also download and print out an official copy of their Medicare card. You can review their Medicare claims within twenty-four hours of processing from their online Medicare account. To sign up, go to www.medicare.gov/account/create-account. You'll need to have their Medicare number and Part A start date available, which is listed on the Medicare card.

HELP APPEAL CLAIM OR COVERAGE DENIALS

You may need to help them appeal denied claims or get prior authorization for a drug they're prescribed or coverage they need. Prior authorization denials will often be reversed on appeal, especially for Medicare Advantage coverage. The MSN lists the timeline and steps for appealing Original Medicare denials; Medicare Advantage appeals start with the insurance company. If you need prior authorization for a drug or procedure, or if that authorization was denied, work with their doctor to submit information about why they need that specific medication or procedure.

GET HELP FROM SHIP

One of the best resources to help family members learn about Medicare coverage and choices for their aging relative is the State Health Insurance Assistance Program (SHIP), which provides free, personalized assistance with Medicare questions. They're a great resource when first signing up for Medicare and dealing with Medicare claims. Their counselors are also some of the best resources for help with open enrollment decisions because they know about the plans available in your area. You can find contact information for your local SHIP at www.shiphelp.org or by calling 1-877-839-2675.

Index

MEDICARE 101